RESUMES
FOR
SALES
AND
MARKETING
CAREERS

Professional Resumes Series

RESUMES FOR SALES AND MARKETING CAREERS

The Editors of
VGM Career Horizons

Second Edition

VGM Career Horizons
NTC/Contemporary Publishing Group

Library of Congress Cataloging-in-Publication Data
Resumes for sales and marketing careers / the editors of
VGM Career Horizons. — 2nd ed. / rev. by Kathy Siebel.
        p.   cm. — (VGM professional resumes series)
    Earlier ed. published under title: Resumes for sales & marketing
careers.
    ISBN 0-8442-6637-X
    1. Résumés (Employment) 2. Sales personnel. 3. Marketing.
I. Siebel, Kathy.   II. VGM Career Horizons (Firm)   III. Title:
Resumes for sales & marketing careers.   IV. Series.
HF5383.R45   1998
650.14′024381—DC21   98-20985
                                                        CIP

ACKNOWLEDGMENT

We would like to acknowledge the assistance of Kathy Siebel in compiling and editing this book.

Published by VGM Career Horizons
A division of NTC/Contemporary Publishing Group, Inc.
4255 West Touhy Avenue, Lincolnwood (Chicago), Illinois 60646-1975 U.S.A.
Copyright © 1998 by NTC/Contemporary Publishing Group, Inc.
Printed in the United States of America
International Standard Book Number: 0-8442-6637-X

18   17   16   15   14   13   12   11   10   9   8   7   6   5   4   3   2   1

CONTENTS

Introduction

Your resume is your first impression on a prospective employer. Though you may be articulate, intelligent, and charming in person, a poor resume may prevent you from ever having the opportunity to demonstrate your interpersonal skills, because a poor resume may prevent you from ever being called for an interview. While few people have ever been hired solely on the basis of their resume, a well-written, well-organized resume can go a long way toward helping you land an interview. Your resume's main purpose is to get you that interview. The rest is up to you and the employer. If you both feel that you are right for the job and the job is right for you, chances are you will be hired.

A resume must catch the reader's attention yet still be easy to read and to the point. Resume styles have changed over the years. Today, brief and focused resumes are preferred. No longer do employers have the patience, or the time, to review several pages of solid type. A resume should be only one page long, if possible, and never more than two pages. Time is a precious commodity in today's business world and the resume that is concise and straightforward will usually be the one that gets noticed

Let's not make the mistake, though, of assuming that writing a brief resume means that you can take less care in preparing it. A successful resume takes time and thought, and if you are willing to make the effort, the rewards are well worth it. Think of your resume as a sales tool with the product being you. You want to sell yourself to a prospective employer. This book is designed to help you prepare a resume that will help you further your career—to land that next job, or first job, or to return to the work force after years of absence. So, read on. Make the effort and reap the rewards that a strong resume can being to your career. Let's get to it!

Chapter One

THE ELEMENTS OF A GOOD RESUME

A winning resume is made of the elements that employers are most interested in seeing when reviewing a job applicant. These basic elements are the essential ingredients of a successful resume and become the actual sections of your resume. The following is a list of elements that may be used in a resume. Some are essential; some are optional. We will be discussing these in this chapter in order to give you a better understanding of each element's role in the makeup of your resume:

1. Heading
2. Objective
3. Work Experience
4. Education
5. Honors
6. Activities
7. Certificates and Licenses
8. Professional Memberships
9. Special Skills
10. Personal Information
11. References

The first step in preparing your resume is to gather together information about yourself and your past accomplishments. Later you will refine this information, rewrite it in the most effective language, and organize it into the most attractive layout. First, let's take a look at each of these important elements individually.

Heading

The heading may seem to be a simple enough element in your resume, but be careful not to take it lightly. The heading should be placed at the top of your resume and should include your name, home address, and telephone numbers. If you can take calls at your current place of business, include your business number, since most employers will attempt to contact you during the business day. If this is not possible, or if you can afford it, purchase an answering machine that allows you to retrieve your messages while you are away from home. This way you can make sure you don't miss important phone calls. Always include your phone number on your resume. It is crucial that when prospective employers need to have immediate contact with you, they can.

Objective

When seeking a particular career path, it is important to list a job objective on your resume. This statement helps employers know the direction that you see yourself heading, so that they can determine whether your goals are in line with the position available. The objective is normally one sentence long and describes your employment goals clearly and concisely. See the sample resumes in this book for examples of objective statements.

The job objective will vary depending on the type of person you are, the field you are in, and the type of goals you have. It can be either specific or general, but it should always be to the point.

In some cases, this element is not necessary, but usually it is a good idea to include your objective. It gives your possible future employer an idea of where you are coming from and where you want to go.

The objective statement is better left out, however, if you are uncertain of the exact title of the job you seek. In such a case, the inclusion of an overly specific objective statement could result in your not being considered for a variety of acceptable positions; you should be sure to incorporate this information in your cover letter, instead.

Work Experience

This element is arguably the most important of them all. It will provide the central focus of your resume, so it is necessary that this section be as complete as possible. Only by examining your work experience in depth can you get to the heart of your accomplishments and present them in a way that demonstrates the strength of your qualifications. Of course, someone just out of school will have less work experience than someone who has been working for a number of years, but the amount of information isn't the most important thing—rather, how it is presented and how it highlights you as a person and as a worker will be what counts.

As you work on this section of your resume, be aware of the need for accuracy. You'll want to include all necessary information about each of your jobs, including job title, dates, employer, city, state, responsibilities, special projects, and accomplishments. Be sure to only list company accomplishments for which you were directly responsible. If you haven't participated in any special projects, that's all right—this area may not be relevant to certain jobs.

The most common way to list your work experience is in *reverse chronological order*. In other words, start with your most recent job and work your way backwards. This way your prospective employer sees your current (and often most important) job before seeing your past jobs. Your most recent position, if the most important, should also be the one that includes the most information, as compared to your previous positions. If you are just out of school, show your summer employment and part-time work, though in this case your education will most likely be more important than your work experience.

The following worksheets will help you gather information about your past jobs.

WORK EXPERIENCE
Job One:

Job Title _____

Dates _____

Employer _____

City, State _____

Major Duties _____

_____

_____

_____

_____

_____

_____

Special Projects _____

_____

_____

_____

Accomplishments _____

_____

_____

_____

_____

_____

_____

_____

Job Two:

Job Title _____

Dates _____

Employer _____

City, State _____

Major Duties _____

_____

_____

_____

_____

_____

_____

Special Projects _____

_____

_____

_____

Accomplishments_____

_____

_____

_____

_____

_____

_____

_____

Job Three:

Job Title _____

Dates _____

Employer _____

City, State _____

Major Duties _____

_____

_____

_____

_____

_____

_____

Special Projects _____

_____

_____

_____

Accomplishments_____

_____

_____

_____

_____

_____

_____

_____

Job Four:

Job Title _____

Dates _____

Employer _____

City, State _____

Major Duties _____

_____

_____

_____

_____

_____

_____

_____

Special Projects _____

_____

_____

_____

Accomplishments_____

_____

_____

_____

_____

_____

_____

_____

Education

Education is the second most important element of a resume. Your educational background is often a deciding factor in an employer's decision to hire you. Be sure to stress your accomplishments in school with the same finesse that you stressed your accomplishments at work. If you are looking for your first job, your education will be your greatest asset, since your work experience will most likely be minimal. In this case, the education section becomes the most important. You will want to be sure to include any degrees or certificates you received, your major area of concentration, any honors, and any relevant activities. Again, be sure to list your most recent schooling first. If you have completed graduate-level work, begin with that and work in reverse chronological order through your undergraduate education. If you have completed an undergraduate degree, you may choose whether to list your high school experience or not. This should be done only if your high school grade-point average was well above average.

The following worksheets will help you gather information for this section of your resume. Also included are supplemental worksheets for honors and for activities. Sometimes honors and activities are listed in a section separate from education, most often near the end of the resume.

EDUCATION

School _____

Major or Area of Concentration _____

Degree _____

Date _____

School _____

Major or Area of Concentration _____

Degree _____

Date _____

Honors

Here, you should list any awards, honors, or memberships in honorary societies that you have received. Usually these are of an academic nature, but they can also be for special achievement in sports, clubs, or other school activities. Always be sure to include the name of the organization honoring you and the date(s) received. Use the worksheet below to help gather your honors information.

HONORS

Honor: _____

Awarding Organization: _____

Date(s): _____

Honor: _____

Awarding Organization: _____

Date(s): _____

Honor: _____

Awarding Organization: _____

Date(s): _____

Honor: _____

Awarding Organization: _____

Date(s): _____

Activities

You may have been active in different organizations or clubs during your years at school; often an employer will look at such involvement as evidence of initiative and dedication. Your ability to take an active role, and even a leadership role, in a group should be included on your resume. Use the worksheet provided to list your activities and accomplishments in this area. In general, you should exclude any organization the name of which indicates the race, creed, sex, age, marital status, color, or nation of origin of its members.

ACTIVITIES

Organization/Activity: _____

Accomplishments: _____

_____

_____

Organization/Activity: _____

Accomplishments: _____

_____

_____

Organization/Activity: _____

Accomplishments: _____

_____

_____

Organization/Activity: _____

Accomplishments: _____

_____

_____

As your work experience increases through the years, your school activities and honors will play less of a role in your resume, and eventually you will most likely only list your degree and any major honors you received. This is due to the fact that, as time goes by, your job performance becomes the most important element in your resume. Through time, your resume should change to reflect this.

Certificates and Licenses

The next potential element of your resume is certificates and licenses. You should list these if the job you are seeking requires them and you, of course, have acquired them. If you have applied for a license, but have not yet received it, use the phrase "application pending."

License requirements vary by state. If you have moved or you are planning to move to another state, be sure to check with the appropriate board or licensing agency in the state in which you are applying for work to be sure that you are aware of all licensing requirements.

Always be sure that all of the information you list is completely accurate. Locate copies of your licenses and certificates and check the exact date and name of the accrediting agency. Use the following worksheet to list your licenses and certificates.

CERTIFICATES AND LICENSES

Name of License: _____

Licensing Agency: _____

Date Issued: _____

Name of License: _____

Licensing Agency: _____

Date Issued: _____

Name of License: _____

Licensing Agency: _____

Date Issued: _____

Professional Memberships

Another potential element in your resume is a section listing professional memberships. Use this section to list involvement in professional associations, unions, and similar organizations. It is to your advantage to list any professional memberships that pertain to the job you are seeking. Be sure to include the dates of your involvement and whether you took part in any special activities or held any offices within the organization. Use the following worksheet to gather your information.

PROFESSIONAL MEMBERSHIPS

Name of Organization: _____

Offices Held: _____

Activities: _____

Date(s): _____

Name of Organization: _____

Offices Held: _____

Activities: _____

Date(s): _____

Name of Organization: _____

Offices Held: _____

Activities: _____

Date(s): _____

Name of Organization: _____

Offices Held: _____

Activities: _____

Date(s): _____

Special Skills

This section of your resume is set aside for mentioning any special abilities you have that could relate to the job you are seeking. This is the part of your resume where you have the opportunity to demonstrate certain talents and experiences that are not necessarily a part of your educational or work experience. Common examples include fluency in a foreign language, or knowledge of a particular computer application.

Special skills can encompass a wide range of your talents—remember to be sure that whatever skills you list relate to the type of work you are looking for.

Personal Information

Some people include "Personal" information on their resumes. This is not generally recommended, but you might wish to include it if you think that something in your personal life, such as a hobby or talent, has some bearing on the position you are seeking. This type of information is often referred to at the beginning of an interview, when it is used as an "ice breaker." Of course, personal information regarding age, marital status, race, religion, or sexual preference should never appear on any resume.

References

References are not usually listed on the resume, but a prospective employer needs to know that you have references who may be contacted if necessary. All that is necessary to include in your resume regarding references is a sentence at the bottom stating, "References are available upon request." If a prospective employer requests a list of references, be sure to have one ready. Also, check with whomever you list to see if it is all right for you to use them as a reference. Forewarn them that they may receive a call regarding a reference for you. This way they can be prepared to give you the best reference possible.

Chapter Two

WRITING YOUR RESUME

*N*ow that you have gathered together all of the information for each of the sections of your resume, it's time to write out each section in a way that will get the attention of whoever is reviewing it. The type of language you use in your resume will affect its success. You want to take the information you have gathered and translate it into a language that will cause a potential employer to sit up and take notice.

Resume writing is not like expository writing or creative writing. It embodies a functional, direct writing style and focuses on the use of action words. By using action words in your writing, you more effectively stress past accomplishments. Action words help demonstrate your initiative and highlight your talents. Always use verbs that show strength and reflect the qualities of a "doer." By using action words, you characterize yourself as a person who takes action, and this will impress potential employers.

The following is a list of verbs commonly used in resume writing. Use this list to choose the action words that can help your resume become a strong one:

administered	introduced
advised	invented
analyzed	maintained
arranged	managed
assembled	met with
assumed responsibility	motivated
billed	negotiated
built	operated
carried out	orchestrated
channeled	ordered
collected	organized
communicated	oversaw
compiled	performed
completed	planned
conducted	prepared
contacted	presented
contracted	produced
coordinated	programmed
counseled	published
created	purchased
cut	recommended
designed	recorded
determined	reduced
developed	referred
directed	represented
dispatched	researched
distributed	reviewed
documented	saved
edited	screened
established	served as
expanded	served on
functioned as	sold
gathered	suggested
handled	supervised
hired	taught
implemented	tested
improved	trained
inspected	typed
interviewed	wrote

Now take a look at the information you put down on the work experience worksheets. Take that information and rewrite it in paragraph form, using verbs to highlight your actions and accomplishments. Let's look at an example, remembering that what matters here is the writing style, and not the particular job responsibilities given in our sample.

WORK EXPERIENCE
Regional Sales Manager

Manager of sales representatives from seven states. Responsible for twelve food chain accounts in the East. In charge of directing the sales force in planned selling toward specific goals. Supervisor and trainer of new sales representatives. Consulting for customers in the areas of inventory management and quality control.

Special Projects: Coordinator and sponsor of annual food industry sales seminar.

Accomplishments: Monthly regional volume went up 25 percent during my tenure while, at the same time, a proper sales/cost ratio was maintained. Customer/company relations improved significantly.

Below is the rewritten version of this information, using action words. Notice how much stronger it sounds.

WORK EXPERIENCE
Regional Sales Manager

Managed sales representatives from seven states. Handled twelve food chain accounts in the eastern United States. Directed the sales force in planned selling towards specific goals. Supervised and trained new sales representatives. Consulted for customers in the areas of inventory management and quality control. Coordinated and sponsored the annual Food Industry Seminar. Increased monthly regional volume 25 percent and helped to improve customer/company relations during my tenure.

Another way of constructing the work experience section is by using actual job descriptions. Job descriptions are rarely written using the proper resume language, but they do include all the information necessary to create this section of your resume. Take the description of one of the jobs your are including on your resume (if you have access to it), and turn it into an action-oriented paragraph. Below is an example of a job description followed by a version of the same description written using action words. Again, pay attention to the style of writing, as the details of your own work experience will be unique.

PUBLIC ADMINISTRATOR I

Responsibilities: Coordinate and direct public services to meet the needs of the nation, state, or community. Analyze problems; work with special committees and public agencies; recommend solutions to governing bodies.

Aptitudes and Skills: Ability to relate to and communicate with people; solve complex problems through analysis; plan, organize, and implement policies and programs. Knowledge of political systems; financial management; personnel administration; program evaluation; organizational theory.

WORK EXPERIENCE
Public Administrator I

Wrote pamphlets and conducted discussion groups to inform citizens of legislative processes and consumer issues. Organized and supervised 25 interviewers. Trained interviewers in effective communication skills.

Now that you have learned how to word your resume, you are ready for the next step in your quest for a winning resume: assembly and layout.

Chapter Three

ASSEMBLY AND LAYOUT

*A*t this point, you've gathered all the necessary information for your resume, and you've rewritten it using the language necessary to impress potential employers. Your next step is to assemble these elements in a logical order and then to lay them out on the page neatly and attractively in order to achieve the desired effect: getting that interview.

Assembly

The order of the elements in a resume makes a difference in its overall effect. Obviously, you would not want to put your name and address in the middle of the resume or your special skills section at the top. You want to put the elements in an order that stresses your most important achievements, not the less pertinent information. For example, if you recently graduated from school and have no full-time work experience, you will want to list your education before you list any part-time jobs you may have held during school. On the other hand, if you have been gainfully employed for several years and currently hold an important position in your company, you will want to list your work experience ahead of your education, which has become less pertinent with time.

There are some elements that are always included in your resume and some that are optional. Following is a list of essential and optional elements:

Essential	Optional
Name	Job Objective
Address	Honors
Phone Number	Special Skills
Work Experience	Professional Memberships
Education	Activities
References Phrase	Certificates and Licenses
	Personal Information

Your choice of optional sections depends on your own background and employment needs. Always use information that will put you and your abilities in a favorable light. If your honors are impressive, then be sure to include them in your resume. If your activities in school demonstrate particular talents necessary for the job you are seeking, then allow space for a section on activities. Each resume is unique, just as each person is unique.

Types of Resumes

So far, our discussion about resumes has involved the most common type—the *reverse chronological* resume, in which your most recent job is listed first and so on. This is the type of resume usually preferred by human resources directors, and it is the one most frequently used. However, in some cases this style of presentation is not the most effective way to highlight your skills and accomplishments.

For someone reentering the work force after many years or someone looking to change career fields, the *functional resume* may work best. This type of resume focuses more on achievement and less on the sequence of your work history. In the functional resume, your experience is presented by what you have accomplished and the skills you have developed in your past work.

A functional resume can be assembled from the same information you collected for your chronological resume. The main difference lies in how you organize this information. Essentially, the work experience section becomes two sections, with your job duties and accomplishments comprising one section and your employer's name, city, state, your position, and the dates employed making up another section. The first section is placed near the top of the resume, just below the job objective section, and can be called *Accomplishments* or *Achievements*. The second section, containing the bare essentials of your employment history, should come after the accomplishments section and can be titled *Work Experience* or *Employment History*. The other sections of your resume remain the same. The work experience section is the only one affected in the functional resume. By placing the section that focuses on your achievements first, you thereby draw attention to these achievements. This puts less emphasis on who you worked for and more emphasis on what you did and what you are capable of doing.

For someone changing careers, emphasis on skills and achievements is essential. The identities of previous employers, which may be unrelated to one's new job field, need to be downplayed. The functional resume accomplishes this task. For someone reentering the work force after many years, a functional resume is the obvious choice. If you lack full-time work experience, you will need to draw attention away from this fact and instead focus on your skills and abilities gained possibly through volunteer activities or part-time work. Education may also play a more important role in this resume.

Which type of resume is right for you will depend on your own personal circumstances. It may be helpful to create a chronological *and* a functional resume and then compare the two to find out which is more suitable. The sample resumes found in this book include both chronological and functional resumes. Use these resumes as guides to help you decide on the content and appearance of your own resume.

Layout

Once you have decided which elements to include in your resume and you have arranged them in an order that makes sense and emphasizes your achievements and abilities, then it is time to work on the physical layout of your resume.

There is no single appropriate layout that applies to every resume, but there are a few basic rules to follow in putting your resume on paper:

1. Leave a comfortable margin on the sides, top, and bottom of the page (usually 1 to 1½ inches).

2. Use appropriate spacing between the sections (usually 2 to 3 line spaces are adequate).

3. Be consistent in the *type* of headings you use for the different sections of your resume. For example, if you capitalize the heading EMPLOYMENT HISTORY, don't use initial capitals and underlining for a heading of equal importance, such as Education.

4. Always try to fit your resume onto one page. If you are having trouble fitting all your information onto one page, perhaps you are trying to say too much. Try to edit out any repetitive or unnecessary information or possibly shorten descriptions of earlier jobs. Be ruthless. Maybe you've included too many optional sections.

CHRONOLOGICAL RESUME

GERALD ROBERT SCAMPI

4890 W. 57th Street
New York, NY 10019
212/555-3678

JOB OBJECTIVE

Vice President of promotion for a communications company.

PROFESSIONAL EXPERIENCE

1996-Present   ATLANTIC RECORDS, New York, NY
Promotion Manager.
Develop and execute all marketing strategies for record promotion in New York, New Jersey, and Massachusetts. Interface with sales department and retail stores to ensure adequate product placement. Attend various company-sponsored sales, marketing, and management seminars.

1987-1996   RSO RECORDS, Miami, FL
Promotion Manager.
Planned all marketing strategies for record promotions in the southeast United States. Worked closely with sales and touring bands to ensure product visibility in the marketplace.

1985-1987   WCFL RADIO, Chicago, IL
On-Air Personality.
Played CHR music. Made TV appearances and public events appearances for the station. Organized and staffed station's news department. Promoted to Music Director after one year.

1980-1985   WGLT RADIO, Atlanta, GA
Program Director, Music Director, and News Director

EDUCATION

COLUMBIA COLLEGE, Chicago, IL
Attended 1979-1980
Studied Audio Engineering

REFERENCES AVAILABLE

FUNCTIONAL RESUME

RENEE GLYKISON
8 E. Western Avenue
Houston, TX 75737
713/555-8098

Job Objective

A position as an assistant sales manager of a publishing company.

Achievements

- Orchestrated market analyses and researched competition for reports to the district manager.
- Identified clients' needs and problems and assured them of personal attention.
- Prepared sales forecasts and sales goals reports.
- Resolved service and billing problems.
- Developed monthly sales plans that identified necessary account maintenance and specific problems that required attention.
- Delivered sales presentations to groups and individuals.
- Maintained daily sales logs and referral logs.
- Identified potential new clients and established new accounts.
- Increased client base by 50%.

Employment History

American National Books, Inc., Houston, TX
Assistant Manager, 1996 to Present

Unico International, Dallas, TX
Sales Representative, 1993 to 1996

Midwest Books, Omaha, NE
Salesperson, 1992 to 1993

Education

Austin College, Austin, TX
B.A. in History, 1992

References Available

Don't let the idea of having to tell every detail about your life get in the way of producing a resume that is simple and straightforward. The more compact your resume, the easier it will be to read and the better an impression it will make for you.

In some cases, the resume will not fit on a single page, even after extensive editing. In such cases, the resume should be printed on two pages so as not to compromise clarity or appearance. Each page of a two-page resume should be marked clearly with your name and the page number, e.g., "Judith Ramirez, page 1 of 2." The pages should then be stapled together.

Try experimenting with various layouts until you find one that looks good to you. Always show your final layout to other people and ask them what they like or dislike about it, and what impresses them most about your resume. Make sure that is what you want most to emphasize. If it isn't, you may want to consider making changes in your layout until the necessary information is emphasized. Use the sample resumes in this book to get some ideas for laying out your resume.

Putting Your Resume in Print

Your resume should be typed or printed on good quality 8½" × 11" bond paper. You want to make as good an impression as possible with your resume; therefore, quality paper is a necessity. If you have access to a word processor with a good printer, or know of someone who does, make use of it. Typewritten resumes should only be used when there are no other options available.

After you have produced a clean original, you will want to make duplicate copies of it. Usually a copy shop is your best bet for producing copies without smudges or streaks. Make sure you have the copy shop use quality bond paper for all copies of your resume. Ask for a sample copy before they run your entire order. After copies are made, check each copy for cleanliness and clarity.

Another more costly option is to have your resume typeset and printed by a printer. This will provide the most attractive resume of all. If you anticipate needing a lot of copies of your resume, the cost of having it typeset may be justified.

Proofreading

After you have finished typing the master copy of your resume and before you go to have it copied or printed, you must thoroughly check it for typing and spelling errors. Have several people read it over just in case you may have missed an error. Misspelled words and typing mistakes will not make a good impression on a prospective employer, as they are a bad reflection on your writing ability and your attention to detail. With thorough and conscientious proofreading, these mistakes can be avoided.

The following are some rules of capitalization and punctuation that may come in handy when proofreading your resume:

Rules of Capitalization

- Capitalize proper nouns, such as names of schools, colleges, and universities, names of companies, and brand names of products.

- Capitalize major words in the names and titles of books, tests, and articles that appear in the body of your resume.

- Capitalize words in major section headings of your resume.

- Do not capitalize words just because they seem important.

- When in doubt, consult a manual of style such as *Words Into Type* (Prentice-Hall), or *The Chicago Manual of Style* (The University of Chicago Press). Your local library can help you locate these and other reference books.

Rules of Punctuation

- Use a comma to separate words in a series.

- Use a semicolon to separate series of words that already include commas within the series.

- Use a semicolon to separate independent clauses that are not joined by a conjunction.

- Use a period to end a sentence.

- Use a colon to show that the examples or details that follow expand or amplify the preceding phrase.

- Avoid the use of dashes.

- Avoid the use of brackets.

- If you use any punctuation in an unusual way in your resume, be consistent in its use.

- Whenever you are uncertain, consult a style manual.

Chapter Four

THE COVER LETTER

*O*nce your resume has been assembled, laid out, and printed to your satisfaction, the next and final step before distribution is to write your cover letter. Though there may be instances where you deliver your resume in person, most often you will be sending it through the mail. Resumes sent through the mail always need an accompanying letter that briefly introduces you and your resume. The purpose of the cover letter is to get a potential employer to read your resume, just as the purpose of your resume is to get that same potential employer to call you for an interview.

Like your resume, your cover letter should be clean, neat, and direct. A cover letter usually includes the following information:

1. Your name and address (unless it already appears on your personal letterhead).

2. The date.

3. The name and address of the person and company to whom you are sending your resume.

4. The salutation ("Dear Mr." or "Dear Ms." followed by the person's last name, or "To Whom It May Concern" if you are answering a blind ad).

5. An opening paragraph explaining why you are writing (in response to an ad, the result of a previous meeting, at the suggestion of someone you both know) and indicating that you are interested in whatever job is being offered.

6. One or two more paragraphs that tell why you want to work for the company and what qualifications and experience you can bring to that company.

7. A final paragraph that closes the letter and requests that you be contacted for an interview. You may mention here that your references are available upon request.

8. The closing ("Sincerely," or "Yours Truly," followed by your signature with your name typed under it).

Your cover letter, including all of the information above, should be no more than one page in length. The language used should be polite, businesslike, and to the point. Do not attempt to tell your life story in the cover letter. A long and cluttered letter will only serve to put off the reader. Remember, you only need to mention a few of your accomplishments and skills in the cover letter. The rest of your information is in your resume. Each and every achievement should not be mentioned twice. If your cover letter is a success, your resume will be read and all pertinent information reviewed by your prospective employer.

Producing the Cover Letter

Cover letters should always be typed individually, since they are always written to particular individuals and companies. Never use a form letter for your cover letter. Cover letters cannot be copied or reproduced like resumes. Each one should be as personal as possible. Of course, once you have written and rewritten your first cover letter to the point where you are satisfied with it, you certainly can use similar wording in subsequent letters.

After you have typed your cover letter on quality bond paper, be sure to proofread it as thoroughly as you did your resume. Again, spelling errors are a sure sign of carelessness, and you don't want that to be a part of your first impression on a prospective employer. Make sure to handle the letter and resume carefully to avoid any smudges, and then mail both your cover letter and resume in an appropriate sized envelope. Be sure to keep an accurate record of all the resumes you send out and the results of each mailing, either in a separate notebook or on individual 3 × 5" index cards.

Numerous sample cover letters appear at the end of the book. Use them as models for your own cover letter or to get an idea of how cover letters are put together. Remember, every one is unique and depends on the particular circumstances of the individual writing it and the job for which he or she is applying.

Now the job of writing your resume and cover letter is complete. About a week after mailing resumes and cover letters to potential employers, you will want to contact them by telephone. Confirm that your resume arrived, and ask whether an interview might be possible. Getting your foot in the door during this call is half the battle of a job search, and a strong resume and cover letter will help you immeasurably.

Chapter Five

SAMPLE RESUMES

This chapter contains dozens of sample resumes for people pursuing a wide variety of jobs and careers.

There are many different styles of resumes in terms of graphic layout and presentation of information. These samples also represent people with varying amounts of education and experience. Use these samples to model your own resume after. Choose one resume, or borrow elements from several different resumes to help you construct your own.

Jeffery Cross

4901 Main Street #242
Evanston, IL 60202
847/555-3877
Cross@aol.com

JOB OBJECTIVE

Seeking a position as a manager of a housewares department of a major department store where I can use my talents as a manager and a salesperson.

ACHIEVEMENTS

Promoted from customer service representative to salesperson to assistant manager in housewares at Marshall Field's. Managed a staff of five, including hiring, job training, and supervision. Helped to reorganize inventory control methods. Assisted customers in choosing housewares and in interior design matters. Combined managerial and sales talents to increase department sales figures.

WORK EXPERIENCE

Marshall Field's, Skokie, IL

Assistant Manager	1994-Present
Salesperson	1992-1994
Customer Service Representative	1991-1992

Peters Hardware, Evanston, IL

Stock Clerk	Summers, 1989-1991

EDUCATION

Oakton Community College, Des Plaines, IL
A.S. in Business, June 1994

REFERENCES AVAILABLE

DANIEL KEYS
548 W. Hollywood Way
Burbank, CA 91505
818/555-9090
Keys @aol.com

PROFESSIONAL OBJECTIVE:

An upper-level management position in the record industry where I can employ my sales, marketing, and promotion experience.

PROFESSIONAL BACKGROUND:

WARNER BROTHERS RECORDS, Burbank, CA
Director, Marketing /Jazz Department, 4/98-Present
Develop and implement strategic marketing plans for new releases and catalog. Produce reissue packages and samplers, both retail and promotional. Create ad copy. Interface with creative services and national/local print and radio. Oversee all aspects of sales. Coordinate promotional activities and chart reports.

I.R.S. RECORDS, Los Angeles, CA
National Sales Manager, 8/94-4/98
West Coast Sales Manager, 9/91-8/94
Increased sales profile, specifically West Coast retailers, one-stops, and racks. Promoted to National Sales Manager where I established sales and promotion programs for company. Coordinated radio/chart reports.

SPECIALTY RECORDS, Scranton, PA
Sales Representative, 1/90-8/94
Handled sales, merchandising, and account servicing for LPs and cassettes. Called on major chains and small independent retailers. Promoted new releases and maintained account inventory.

TOWER RECORDS, Los Angeles, CA
Manager, 8/89-1/90
Handled sales, merchandising, customer service, product selection and ordering, personnel management and supervision for a full-line retail outlet.

MCA RECORDS DISTRIBUTION, Universal City, CA
Sales Representative, 9/83-8/89
Promoted and sold MCA product to Los Angeles and surrounding counties. Designed in-store window displays. Coordinated media advertising support programs.

EDUCATION:

Berkeley University, Berkeley, CA
B.A., Liberal Arts, June 1981

CAROL GHERKIN

4432 W. Simpson Street
Minneapolis, MN 44515

Telephone: (612) 555-4342
Fax: (612) 555-4343

JOB OBJECTIVE:

Seeking a sales position with a pharmaceutical company that services hospitals where I can utilize my education, my communication skills, and my sales experience.

EXPERIENCE:

Sales Representative, PHARMED, INC., St. Paul, MN, 2/98 to Present
Demonstrate and explain new drugs to physicians. Handle follow-ups and updates on previous product. Increased sales 30% in my first two years. Help train new sales representatives.

Sales Trainee, HOSPO SUPPLY COMPANY, Edina, MN, 4/97 to 2/98
Determined which drugs were necessary for stocking hospital supply rooms. Handled stocking for previously established orders. Increased staff awareness of new products.

EDUCATION:

M.S., University of Minnesota, Chemistry, 1997
B.S., Iowa State University, Chemistry, 1995

SEMINARS:

"Presenting New Drugs to In-Office Physicians," Sales and Marketing Professionals' Association, 1997

HONORS:

Raymond Johnson Chemistry Award, 1997
Phi Beta Kappa, 1995
Dean's List, 1994, 1995

ACTIVITIES:

Chemistry Club, 1997
Biology Club, 1994-1995

REFERENCES AVAILABLE

MARION ZARET
3333 W. 57th Street
Brooklyn, NY 12909
847/555-2323
847/555-4999

OBJECTIVE

Public relations director for a major beverage company

WORK EXPERIENCE

Coca Cola, Inc., New York, NY
National Sales Manager   1997 to Present
Account Manager   1995 to 1997
Assistant Account Manager 1994 to 1995
Personnel Assistant   1992 to 1994
Receptionist   1990 to 1992

Managed a sales staff that included account managers and sales representatives. Monitored the effectiveness of a national distribution network. Represented company to clients and retailers in order to present new products. Organized and planned convention displays and strategy. Oversaw all aspects of sales/marketing budget. Designed and executed direct-mail program that identified marketplace needs and new options for products. Conceived ads, posters, and point-of-purchase materials for products. Initiated and published a monthly newsletter that was distributed to current and potential customers.

EDUCATION

American University, White Plains, NY
B.A. in English, 1989

SEMINARS

American Marketing Association Seminars, 1995-1998
Coca Cola Internal Sales Workshops, 1996-1998
Soft Drink Industry Conventions

REFERENCES

On request

PEDRO C. GONZALES

7 E. Pullman Road
Chicago, IL 60634
312/555-4560

Objective:	A position as a sales representative in which I employ my sales and communication skills.
Work History:	<u>Belwin-Mills Inc.</u>, Chicago, IL Salesperson, 1997 to Present Sell sheet music to retail businesses. Named top salesperson of 1997. Maintain excellent customer relations by identifying and meeting customer needs. Train new sales representatives and advise them on effective selling techniques. <u>Fuller Brush Company</u>, Aurora, IL Salesperson, 1992 - 1997 Sold products for the home in the south suburban Chicago area. Increased territory sales by 65% in five years. Demonstrated and planned specific uses for household products. Maintained constant contact with accounts.
Education:	<u>Fuller Brush Training Course</u>, Aurora, IL Summer 1992 <u>Barton Technical High School</u>, Chicago, IL Graduated 1992 Tennis Team, Co-captain
References:	Available upon request

Rhoda Browne

7 S. Robinson Drive
Des Plaines, IL 60018

847/555-5401
847/555-8032

EDUCATION

M.B.A. in Marketing
University of Illinois, Champaign-Urbana
Degree awarded June 1997

B.S. in Finance
University of Colorado, Boulder, CO
Degree awarded May 1995

HONORS

Summa Cum Laude, 1997
Dean's List, 1994, 1995

WORK HISTORY

HOPPER MANUFACTURING, Skokie, IL

8/97 to Present	Administrative Assistant/Sales Department Assist account executives with general correspondence, data entry, and sales proposals. Set up and staff displays at industry trade shows.
Summer 1996	Sales Trainee Assisted with billing, orders, shipping, and inventory.

REFERENCES

Available on request.

DONALD E. THOMPSON
1314 W. Dundee Road
Buffalo Grove, IL 60006
847/555-3909

Job Objective:	Computer Sales

Experience: **Microtech Computers, Northbrook, IL**
Account Executive, 4/89 to Present
Handle sales accounts for Northwest suburban area. Have expanded customer base by 25% during my tenure. Conduct field visits to solve customer problems. Maintain daily contact with customers by telephone to ensure good customer/company relations. Wrote product information fliers and distributed them through direct mail program.

IBM, Chicago, IL
Technical Support Specialist, 9/81 to 4/89
Installed and maintained operating system. Defined and oversaw network lists and tables. Coordinated problem resolution with phone companies. Performance tuned subsystems and networks. Planned and installed new hardware and programming techniques.

IBM, Chicago, IL
Systems Analyst, 2/70 to 9/81
Documented procedures for mechanization of payroll department. Created standards and procedures for main accounting system. Coordinated requirements meeting with production department on new inventory system. Developed test procedures for reverification of new application. Developed distribution lists, user IDs, and standards for electronic mail system.

Education: **Northwestern University, Evanston, IL**

M.S. in Mathematics, 1970
Graduated with honors

B.S. in Chemistry, 1968
Dean's List
Seabrook Scholarship

Page 1 of 2

Donald E. Thompson -2-

Affiliations: Computer Sales Association
Illinois Business Chapter

Seminars: Microtech Sales Seminars
IBM Technical Workshops

References available on request

SHAWANA HODGES
5678 N. Riverside Drive
Burbank, CA 91505
818/555-8989
Hodges@aol.com

CAREER OBJECTIVE: Sales representative for an office supplies company.

ACHIEVEMENTS:

~Handled price quotations, information on product line, customer inquiries on shipments and special orders.

~Assisted sales manager in establishing and streamlining standard office procedures.

~Arranged travel and transportation, hotel and scheduling of seminars and meetings.

~Drafted monthly reports on sales procedures and profit margins.

~Managed computerization of office records.

~Routed editing duties and proofreading responsibilities.

~Edited and proofread interoffice memos and a weekly department newsletter.

~Supervised two student interns.

WORK HISTORY:

Sanco Office Supplies, Ltd., Burbank, CA
Executive Secretary to Sales Manager, 1995 to Present

Popular Artists Management, Los Angeles, CA
Secretary to Manager of Publications, 1993 to 1995

EDUCATION:

Pasadena College, Pasadena, CA
B.S. in Marketing, 1997
Evening Division

Commercial School of Business, Los Angeles, CA
Completed advanced secretarial course.

SKILLS: WordPerfect 6.1, PageMaker, Excel, Lotus 1-2-3

REFERENCES: Available on request

HANNAH GOLDSTEIN

1800 W. Pico Street
Santa Monica, CA 90110
213/555-8938
E-mail: Gold@aol.com

Job Objective

A marketing/promotion position in the entertainment industry where I can utilize my communication skills, contacts, and industry knowledge.

Work Experience

TBC MARKETING, Burbank, CA
Independent Marketing, 1/98 to Present
Coordinate stock with regional distributors. Generate exposure and interest at local retail stores and one-stops in conjunction with local and regional airplay. Suggest supplemental marketing strategies based on airplay, sales, and percentage penetration.

HITS MAGAZINE, Van Nuys, CA
National Marketing Coordinator, 4/96 to 1/98
Sold charts and tracking information to radio, artist management, and record labels. Handled tracking for all accounts on charting product. Interacted with radio accounts weekly regarding early chart information.

CASHBOX MAGAZINE, Los Angeles, CA
Regional Sales Representative, 4/93 to 4/96
Managed and developed West Coast territory for Cashbox Service Network. Provided chart information, including bullet criteria, points, sales/airplay ratios to independent marketing companies and management. Serviced retail accounts and created new marketing strategies for product tracking services.

PARKER MANUFACTURING, Flint, MI
Sales Representative, 7/89 to 4/93
Negotiated and sold contract repairs on industrial equipment. Wrote daily technical reports on product movement and inventory. Consistently met and exceeded quarterly sales quotas.

Education

Michigan State University, Grand Rapids, MI
B.A., Communications, June 1989

References

Available on request.

HENRY JAZZINSKI
300 Big Malle Road
Dallas, TX 84038
214/555-8888 (Daytime)
214/555-3839 (Evening)

OBJECTIVE

A management position in the sales and marketing field.

ACHIEVEMENTS

Sales

- Increased watch sales from $3 million to $12 million during the past six years.
- Introduced new and existing product lines through presentation to marketing directors and major manufacturers.
- Developed 15 new accounts.
- Supervised 5 sales agencies throughout the United States and Canada.

Marketing

- Developed new products expanding from watches to other accessories that resulted in increased sales.
- Researched the watch market in order to coordinate product line with current fashion trends.
- Increased company's share of the market through improved quality products.

WORK HISTORY

Culture Shock Watch Company, Dallas, TX
Vice President of Sales and Marketing, 1989 to Present

Nabisco Food Company, San Francisco, CA
Sales & Product Food Manager, 1984 to 1989

Avis, Inc., Los Angeles, CA
Sales Representative, 1979 to 1984

Page 1 of 2

Henry Jazzinski
Page 2 of 2

EDUCATION

<u>University of Southern California</u>, Los Angeles, CA
B.S. in Business Administration, 1978

SEMINARS

Dallas Sales & Marketing Conference, 1997, 1998
National Marketing Association Convention, 1992-1996

REFERENCES AVAILABLE

SANDRA SORENSON

3201 W. Oerno Street
Apartment 23
Pittsburgh, PA 38901
412/555-9302
412/555-4209

E-Mail: sspr@aol.com

JOB SOUGHT: Public relations director for the marketing division of a major candy manufacturer.

EXPERIENCE: <u>Public Relations</u>
~Represented company to clients and retailers in order to present new products.
~Assisted in design of company web site.
~Organized and planned convention displays and strategy.
~Designed and executed direct mail campaign that identified marketplace needs.
~Developed new options for products.

<u>Management</u>
~Managed a sales/marketing staff that included account managers and sales representatives.
~Monitored and studied the effectiveness of a national distribution network.
~Oversaw all aspects of sales/marketing budget.

<u>Development</u>
~Conceived ads, posters, and point-of-purchase materials for products.
~Initiated and published a monthly newsletter that was distributed to current and potential customers.

WORK HISTORY: <u>Redboy Peanut Crunch</u>, Pittsburgh, PA
National Sales Manager, 1997-present
Account Manager, 1995-1997
Assistant Account Manager, 1994-1995
Personnel Assistant, 1992-1994
Receptionist, 1990-1992

EDUCATION: B.A. in English, 1989
University of Pennsylvania, Harrisburg, PA

SEMINARS: American Marketing Association Seminars, 1995-1998

SKILLS: Computer literacy in BASIC and FORTRAN. Knowledge of WordPerfect 6.1 and dBASE III.

REFERENCES: Available on request

Melanie A. Maloney
1200 Puerta Del Sol
Chatsworth, CA 92203

714/555-6789

Objective:

Full-time sales position that will allow me to use my sales, customer service, and design skills to benefit an established jewelry store.

Overview:

- Several years of experience selling jewelry
- Excellent customer service record
- Ability to resolve customer complaints to the satisfaction of customers and employers
- Proven record of generating repeat business by establishing rapport with customers
- Ability to design creative, effective jewelry displays
- Attention to detail in entering computer data and managing inventory

Work Experience:

Stacey's Jewelers, Chatsworth, CA
Sales Associate, 1/98 to Present

Eddy Gems, Glendale, CA
Sales Clerk, 4/95 to 12/97

Jones Day Care, Tempe, AZ
Art Teacher, 2/93 to 4/95

Parker Hardware, Robeson, AZ
Cashier, 5/91 to 2/93

Education:

Tempe College, Tempe, AZ
B.A. in Art, January, 1993

Honors:

Tempe Honor Society, 1993
Velma G. Lydeckker Art Award, 1992

Special Skills:

Fluent in Spanish
Hands-on computer experience using FORTRAN

References:

Available on request

ELVIRA WASHINGTON
453 Franklin Avenue
San Diego, CA 94890
619/555-3489

Career Objective

A management position in marketing where I can utilize my promotion and public relations experience.

Work Experience

JUST PASTA, INC., San Diego, CA
Marketing Director, 1996 to Present
Direct a successful marketing campaign for a restaurant chain. Initiate and maintain a positive working relationship with radio and print media. Implement marketing strategies to increase sales at less profitable outlets. Administer a training program for store managers and staff.

GREAT IDEAS CARPET CLEANING COMPANY, Dallas, TX
Marketing Representative, 1992 to 1996
Demonstrated carpet cleaners in specialty and department stores. Reported customer reactions to manufacturers. Designed flier and advertising to promote products. Made frequent calls to retail outlets.

REBO CHIPS, Chicago, IL
Assistant Sales Manager, 1987 to 1992
Handled both internal and external areas of sales and marketing, including samples, advertising, and pricing. Served as company sales representative and sold potato chips to retail outlets.

Education

UNIVERSITY OF ILLINOIS AT CHICAGO, Chicago, IL
B.A. in Marketing, 1987

Seminars

San Diego State Marketing Workshop, 1998
Sales and Marketing Association Seminars, 1994

References Available

Mary Alice Moore
3230 Alsip Court, #3C
Milwaukee, WI 53100

419/555-8908
moore@aol.com

Objective

Marketing representative for a major U.S. airline.

Experience

Midwest Airlines, Inc. Milwaukee, WI
Sales Representative, 2/98 to Present

Sell reservations for domestic flights, hotels, and car rentals. Market travel packages through travel agencies. Negotiate airline and hotel discounts for customers. Devise itineraries and solve customers' travel-related problems.

Travel in the Main, Evanston, IL
Travel Agent, 6/90 to 2/98

Handled customer reservations for airlines, hotels, and car rentals. Advised customers on competitive travel packages and prices. Interacted with all major airlines, hotel chains, and car rental companies.

Education

University of Wisconsin, Beloit, WI
B.A. in Anthropology, 1976

Skills

Hands-on experience using most travel-related computer systems, including Apollo. Working knowledge of German, French, and Polish.

References

On request

JEREMY S. PANDY
1441 S. Goebert
Providence, RI 00231
401/555-1234
401/555-3782

Objective

President of a U. S. publishing corporation where I can apply my management, promotion, and sales experience.

Employment History

JOHNSON PUBLISHING CORPORATION, Providence, RI
VICE PRESIDENT, 1990 - 1998

Promoted from sales manager to vice president of advertising after three years. Managed all phases of publishing properties including:

> *Furniture Magazine*
> *Home Improvement Weekly*
> *Scuba Digest*
> *Travel Age Magazine*
> *Pharmacy News*

Established and developed the first newspaper advertising mat service in the furniture industry. Increased distributors and retailers using this service by 55% in three years. Improved the effectiveness and volume of all retail advertising.

REBUS PUBLISHING COMPANY, Boston, MA
ADVERTISING MANAGER, 1981 - 1990

Serviced and developed accounts throughout the eastern United States. Handled advertising for publications in the restaurant industry. Increased sales in my territories every year by at least 21%.

TIME MAGAZINE, New York, NY
ASSISTANT ADVERTISING PROMOTION MANAGER, 1977 -1981

Spearheaded original promotion program that increased revenue 33% in two years. Developed new markets. Helped to improve customer/company relations.

ROYAL CROWN COLA CORPORATION, Chicago, IL
DIVISION SALES MANAGER, 1974 - 1977

Promoted from salesperson to sales manager after one year. Organized sampling campaigns and in-store and restaurant displays. Directed bottlers' cooperative advertising and point-of-purchase displays.

Page 1 of 2

Education

DRAKE UNIVERSITY, Des Moines, IA
Graduated Phi Beta Kappa
Top 5% of class

Professional Affiliations

Rocking Chair, social and professional organization of the furniture industry
President, 1998 - Present

Beverage Association of America
Board of Directors

Publishers Association
Advisory Committee

References

Available upon request

MICHELLE CRUMLEY
2316 Sherman Avenue, #3B
Evanston, IL 60201
(847) 555-4727

EDUCATION:	Northwestern University, Evanston, IL
Bachelor of Science in Economics
Expected June 1999
GPA: 3.45
HONORS:	Phi Beta Kappa
Dean's List, Seven Quarters
Owen L. Coon Award, Honorable Mention
ACTIVITIES:	President, Activities and Organizations Board
Wa-Mu Show
Captain, Soccer Team
Freshman Advisor
WORK EXPERIENCE:	Shand Morihand Insurance Company, Evanston, IL
Marketing Intern, 1998
Assisted marketing staff in the areas of research, demographics, and sales forecasts designed to identify new customers and direct promotion.

Northwestern University, Evanston, IL
Student Assistant, Registrar's Office, 1997 - 1998
Processed transcript requests. Entered registrations on the computer. Provided students with basic information regarding registration. |
| SKILLS: | Knowledge of French and Russian
Experience with WordPerfect 6.1 and Microsoft Works |
| REFERENCES: | Available on request |

DIANA FAGEN THOMPSON

8000 E. Fifth Avenue
Silver Springs, MD 04890
410-555-4988

Objective: A management position in sales or marketing.

Work History: **Interco, Washington, DC**
Regional Sales Manager, 1993 - Present
Manage sales of all product lines in eastern markets for a
leading manufacturer of cotton products. Represent five
corporate divisions of the company, with sales in excess
of $2 million annually. Direct and motivate a sales force
of 12 in planned selling to achieve company goals.

Robertson Company, Miami, FL
District Manager, 1988 - 1993
Acted as sales representative for the Miami metropolitan
area. Built both wholesale and dealer distribution substantially
during my tenure. Developed monthly sales plans that identified
necessary account maintenance and specific problems that
required attention.

Western Office Products, Sarasota, FL
Assistant Sales Manager, 1985 - 1988
Handled both internal and external areas of sales and marketing,
including samples, advertising, and pricing. Served as company
sales representative and sold a variety of office supplies to
retail stores.

Education: Miami University, Miami, FL
B.A. in English, 1983

Seminars: American Sales Association Seminars, 1995 - 1998

References: Available on request

TYRELL JACOBS, III
4504 Bloomfeld Avenue
Westchester, NY 12090
718/555-3849

JOB OBJECTIVE: A management-level sales position within the plastics industry.

**PROFESSIONAL
EXPERIENCE:**

Clear Plastics, Inc., Brooklyn, NY
Sales Manager, 1995 - present
Sell custom designed point-of-purchase elements and product displays. Research target areas and develop new account leads. Research and determine advertising in national publications. Make sales presentations to potential customers. Participate in plastics industry trade shows.

Westchester Tractor Company, Westchester, NY
District Sales Manager, 1991 - 1995
Planned successful sales strategies in order to identify and develop new accounts. Supervised seven sales representatives. Researched and analyzed market conditions to seek out new customers. Wrote monthly sales reports.

Brooklyn Freight Company, Brooklyn, NY
Account Executive, 1988 - 1991
Managed accounts in the New York metropolitan area. Expanded customer base 30% in four years. Monitored customer satisfaction with product and service. Developed training program for new hires.

EDUCATION: Harvard University, Boston, MA
M.B.A. with honors, 1987

Drake University, Des Moines, IA
B.A. in Accounting, 1984

**PROFESSIONAL
MEMBERSHIPS:**   Brooklyn Sales Association, 1996 - present
New York Merchants Group, 1991 - present

REFERENCES: Available on request

JULIUS T. SHATTACK
45 E. 45th Street #414
Minneapolis, MN 50290
612/555-3490

JOB OBJECTIVE

A position as a sales/marketing representative for a manufacturer of musical instruments.

PROFESSIONAL ACHIEVEMENTS

Sales

*Established and maintained an excellent relationship with more than 100 accounts in the musical instrument industry.
*Resolved customer complaints promptly.
*Provided customers with detailed information on products and replacement parts.
*Named salesperson of the month six times.

Marketing

*Demonstrated to customers the value of quality purchases.
*Researched industry competition to refine and strengthen marketing techniques.
*Projected success of new products through surveys and questionnaires.

WORK HISTORY

Roland Corporation, Minneapolis, MN
Sales Representative, 1997 - present

Twin Cities Electronics, St. Paul, MN
Salesperson, 1994 - 1997

EDUCATION

Milton Community College, Edina, MN
A.S. Degree in Business, May 1994

REFERENCES AVAILABLE

David Terrence Johnson
5656 W. Ogden Avenue
La Grange, IL 60189
847/555-1828
847/555-2020

Objective

Full-time, management level sales and marketing position

Professional Achievements

Sales
- Introduced new and existing product lines through presentations to major clients.
- Increased sales from $27 million to $50 million in five years.
- Initiated and developed nine new accounts.
- Supervised five sales agencies throughout the United States.

Marketing

- Researched computer market in order to coordinate product line with current public tastes and buying trends.
- Developed new approaches to marketing software products, including in-store displays and advertising.
- Organized and planned convention displays and strategies.

Employment History

Ranco Computer Company, Chicago, IL
Sales and Marketing Manager, 1995 - present

Unico, Melrose Park, IL
Product Coordinator, 1985 -1995

Torvis Electrical Supply, Canoga Falls, NY
Sales Representative, 1980 -1985

Page 1 of 2

David Terrence Johnson   -2-

Education

New York University, New York, NY
B.S., June 1985
Major: Business Administration
Minor: Computer Science

References

Available on request

VONDA MAPLES

7777 W. Devon Avenue   312/555-8900
Chicago, IL 60646   312/555-7200

OBJECTIVE: Sales Manager

**WORK
EXPERIENCE:**   Pier One Imports, Chicago, IL
                        Sales Coordinator, 1997 to Present
                        Manage ten field representatives. Disseminate information
                        on company policies, sales goals, and strategies. Co-design
                        full-color catalog. Place advertising in major trade publications.
                        Promote products at trade shows. Maintain inventory status
                        reports and personnel records.

                        Auburn Publishing Company, Lincolnwood, IL
                        Distribution Assistant, 1990 to 1997
                        Developed new distribution outlets through cold-calls and
                        follow-up visits. Increased distribution in my district by 45%
                        over a three-year period. Coordinated a direct-mail program
                        that increased magazine subscriptions 120%.

                        Canon Company, Atlanta, GA
                        Sales Representative, 1985 to 1990
                        Sold and serviced office copiers to businesses and schools in
                        the greater Atlanta area. Maintained good customer relations
                        through frequent calls and visits. Identified potential customers.

EDUCATION: Atlanta University, Atlanta, GA
                        B.A. in Communications, June 1985

**PROFESSIONAL
MEMBERSHIPS:**   National Association of Importers
                        Rogers Park Community Association
                        Lion's Club

REFERENCES: Available on request.

Grisette Allman
1202 W. North Avenue
Chicago, IL 60645

312/555-8909

Overview:

Experienced salesperson with managerial background. Seeking a position in sales management with a major retailer that will allow me to use and expand my sales and marketing skills.

Work History:

GRANDY'S SHOES, Chicago, IL   Assistant Manager   4/97-Present
        Serve as assistant manager of a quality shoe store with partial supervision of a staff of six. Track customers' buying habits and analyze market trends. Handle promotion and mailings for special sales and in-store events. Open and close store on weekends, manage cash and bank deposits.

FLAHERTY JEWELERS, Arlington Heights, IL   Salesperson   1/90-4/97
        Sold jewelry at a fine jewelry store. Answered customer questions regarding product. Tracked inventory on computer. Stocked inventory within the store. Kept store clean and orderly. Trained new hires on sales techniques and use of cash register. Handled returns and orders from distributors. Designed displays for store.

CANON COMPANY, Atlanta, GA   Salesperson   8/85-1/90
        Sold copiers to schools and businesses in the greater Atlanta area. Explained product features and terms of sale at on-site sales presentations. Expanded customer base through intensive cold calling in person and over the phone.

Education:

Atlanta Community College, Atlanta, GA
Attended two years, majoring in Business

Central High School, Marietta, GA
Graduated 1985
Winner, Math Award

References Available

Kenneth Thomas Parker

1400 Lake Shore Drive
Chicago, IL 60601
312/555-1212 (Days)
312/555-2901 (Evenings)

JOB OBJECTIVE

Sales manager for a company that manufactures sporting goods.

PROFESSIONAL EXPERIENCE

Sales and Promotion

- Made cold calls and visits to sporting goods retailers that resulted in new accounts.
- Visited and serviced existing accounts to encourage continued sales.
- Advised customers on options available to meet a wide range of product needs.
- Handled dealer requests for information and sample products.

Marketing

- Researched competitive products in order to evaluate competitors' strengths and weaknesses.
- Planned a marketing strategy that resulted in a significant increase in accounts.
- Maintained demographic data in order to ascertain buyer profile.

EMPLOYMENT HISTORY

Wilson Sporting Goods, Inc., Morton Grove, IL
Assistant Sales Manager, 1995 - present
Sales Representative, 1993 - 1995

Chambers & Company, Chicago, IL
Marketing Assistant, 1992

Page 1 of 2

KENNETH THOMAS PARKER - 2

EMPLOYMENT HISTORY (cont.)

<u>Morey Mages Sporting Goods</u>, Skokie, IL
Salesperson, 1990 - 1992

<u>Bennigan's Restaurant</u>, Lincolnwood, IL
Waiter, 1989 - 1990

EDUCATION

<u>University of Illinois at Chicago</u>, Chicago, IL
B.A. in Marketing, 1992

HONORS

Phi Beta Kappa, 1992
Dean's List, 1990 - 1992
Seymour G. Reim Marketing Scholarship, 1990, 1991
President, Student Activities Board, 1992

SPECIAL SKILLS

Knowledge of Excel, PowerPoint, and WordPerfect 6.1

REFERENCES

Available on request.

IRA T. SIMPSON
76 N. Washington Blvd.
Houston, TX 72009
714/555-4890

GOAL: A position as a sales representative that involves direct sales and account management.

WORK EXPERIENCE:

R&G Sugar, Inc., Houston, TX
Salesperson, 1997 - Present
Sell refined sugar products to retail businesses. Named top salesperson of 1996. Maintain good customer relations by identifying customer needs. Train new sales representatives and advise them on effective selling techniques.

Popson Camera Company, Milwaukee, WI
Salesperson, 1992 - 1997
Sold cameras to retail outfits in the south suburban Milwaukee area. Increased territory sales by 85% in five years. Planned and demonstrated specific uses for products in various offices. Maintained contact with accounts.

EDUCATION:

Popson Sales Training Course, Milwaukee, WI
Summer 1992

Cobert Technical High School, West Allis, WI
Graduated 1991
Football Team, Co-captain

REFERENCES: Available on request

JANE WIGGINS

1814 N. Seminola Avenue
Cleveland, OH 47889
216/555-3400(Daytime)
216/555-2910(Evenings)

CAREER OBJECTIVE

To become a sales representative for an office supplies
manufacturer.

EMPLOYMENT HISTORY

Tempo Office Supply Company, Cleveland, OH
Executive Secretary to Sales Manager, 1995-Present

Assist sales manager in various office activities and procedures.
Handle price quotations, information on product line, customer
inquiries on shipments and special orders. Arrange travel and
transportation, and scheduling of seminars and meetings.
Draft monthly reports on sales procedures and profit margins.
Manage computerization of the office records.

James Plastics, St. Louis, MO
Secretary to Manager of Publications, 1993-1995

Arranged conferences for the department. Dealt directly with
staff members in a variety of manners including routing editing
duties and proofreading responsibilities. Edited and proofread
interoffice memos and a weekly department newsletter. Arranged
for printing and distribution. Supervised two student interns.

EDUCATION

Cleveland University, Cleveland, OH
B.S. in Marketing, 1997

St. Louis School of Business, St. Louis, MO
A.S. in Office Technology, 1992

SPECIAL SKILLS

Proficiency in WordPerfect 6.1, PowerPoint, and Excel
Knowledge of Spanish

REFERENCES

Available on Request

Lynda S. Woods
3302 Harbor Drive, #45
Ft. Lauderdale, FL 33020
305-555-8903

Work Experience

<u>South Florida Boat Company</u>, Miami, FL
District Sales Manager, 1996 - present

Planned successful strategies to identify and develop new accounts. Increased sales by at least 20% each year (45% in 1988). Researched and analyzed market conditions in order to seek out new customers. Developed weekly and monthly sales strategies. Supervised a sales staff of eight.

<u>Miami Industrial Supply</u>, Miami, FL
Account Executive, 1994 - 1996

Responsible for south Florida territory. Developed 23 new accounts during a two-year period. Resolved customer complaints. Provided feedback to production and shipping departments that improved customer service. Rewrote product catalog. Updated customer database. Implemented new system for standard reorders. Trained department clerical assistants.

<u>Harrison Pany, Inc.</u>, Denver, CO
Sales Representative, 1993 - 1994

Sold and serviced office copiers to businesses and schools throughout the greater Denver area. Designed and disbursed customer satisfaction surveys. Attended trade shows to analyze and select new product. Expanded customer base through successful direct-mail marketing campaign.

Education

University of Colorado, Boulder, CO
B.A., June 1993
Major: Economics
Minor: Music

Page 1 of 2

Professional Memberships

South Florida Sales Association, Treasurer, 1998 - present
Miami Chamber of Commerce, 1996 - present

References

Available on request.

REBA MALONEY

331 Maple Avenue
Seattle, WA 99449

206/555-3898 (Home)
206/555-4444 (Work)

OBJECTIVE:

A management position at a dress shop.

WORK EXPERIENCE:

AVON DRESS SHOP, Seattle, WA
Assistant Manager, 1994 to Present

Sell dresses, wait on customers, advise on style, handle special orders and mail orders, and take care of returned merchandise. Assist in design of window displays. Oversee the placement of ads for major advertising campaigns. Represent store at conventions.

QUALITY BOUTIQUE, Tall Oaks, CA
Salesperson, 1993 to 1994

Sold accessories to customers, filled special orders, organized and arranged inventory. Handled customer returns and special requests. Designed window displays.

EDUCATION:

TALL OAKS HIGH SCHOOL, Tall Oaks, WA

Graduated in June 1994
Ranked 14 in class of 300
Member of tennis team

REFERENCES:

Provided on request

GINA CAROL STONE
5001 Lincoln Drive #2
Marlton, NJ 08053
609/555-1200
609/555-3893

OBJECTIVE: Sales manager of a paper products company.

PROFESSIONAL
EXPERIENCE: HARRISON PAPER COMPANY, Philadelphia, PA
                         District Sales Manager, 1994 - Present

                         Plan successful strategies in order to identify and develop new
                         accounts. Have increased sales by at least 20% each year
                         (50% in 1997). Research and analyze market conditions in
                         order to seek out new customers. Develop weekly and monthly
                         sales strategies. Supervise seven sales representatives.

                         DANIEL P. MILLER & COMPANY, Trenton, NJ
                         Sales Representative, 1987 - 1994

                         Developed and managed new territories. Built sales through
                         calls on retailers and wholesalers. Developed creative
                         techniques for increasing product sales. Maintained current
                         knowledge of competitive products. Wrote weekly and monthly
                         sales reports.

                         SAMMY'S BEST BURGER COMPANY, Newark, NJ
                         Assistant to Sales Manager, 1980 -1987

                         Handled both internal and external areas of sales and
                         marketing, including samples, advertising, and pricing.
                         Served as company sales representative and sold a variety
                         of products to retail stores.

EDUCATION: NEW JERSEY STATE UNIVERSITY, Trenton, NJ
                         B.S. in Business, 1979
                         Graduated top 10% of class
                         Recipient of Floyd T. Harper Scholarship

SPECIAL
SKILLS: Knowledge of Russian
                         WordPerfect 6.1
                         Excel

REFERENCES: On request

Ivan P. Lins
24 E. Saginaw
Crystal Lake, IL 60203
(847) 555-3894

Job Objective

A position as a marketing manager where I can utilize my knowledge and experience in sales and marketing.

Relevant Accomplishments

- Managed sales of all product lines in midwestern markets for a leading maker of textiles.
- Represented five corporate divisions of the company with sales in excess of $3 million annually.
- Directed and motivated a sales force of 12 sales representatives in planned selling toward specific goals.
- Built wholesale and dealer distribution substantially as district manager.
- Handled both internal and external areas of sales and marketing for an office supply manufacturer.
- Oversaw all aspects of samples, advertising, and marketing.
- Maintained good customer relations with retail stores.

Employment History

Robeau Industries, Chicago, IL
Regional Sales Manager, 2/95 to present

Carolina Company, Elgin, IL
District Sales Manager, 5/90 to 2/95

Super Office Company, St. Louis, MO
Assistant to the Sales Manager, 8/86 to 5/90

Page 1 of 2

Ivan P. Lins
Page 2

Education

University of Michigan, Ann Arbor, MI
B.A. in Business Administration, 1985
Major: Marketing
Minor: Spanish

Seminars

National Management Association Seminar, 1994
Chicago University Seminars, 1997, 1998

Professional Memberships

Sales and Marketing Association of Chicago
National Association of Market Developers

References

References available on request

STEVEN TYLER

17001 E. Riverside Drive   818/555-3728 (Day)
Burbank, CA 91505   818/555-9000 (Evening)

OBJECTIVE

Marketing management.

RELEVANT ACHIEVEMENTS

Marketing

- Implemented various programs including product visuals, giveaways, and delivery of presentations.
- Conceived and developed creative product promotions.
- Designed unique advertising with innovative placements, including billboards, trade publications, and newspapers.
- Administered advertising budget.
- Represented company to both industry and media.

Sales

- Exceeded revenue goals by 41% this last year.
- Set annual sales records in 1997 with revenues of $55 million.
- Administered a $125 million advertising budget.

Management

- Restructured Paradise Vacations achieving #1 position in sales for the western United States.
- Designed and wrote new policy manuals and job descriptions for all departments.
- Trained staff and managers in order to increase productivity.
- Directed the sales force in achieving and exceeding sales goals.

EMPLOYMENT HISTORY

Paradise Vacations, Burbank, CA
Senior Vice President, 1996-Present

Western Airlines, San Diego, CA
Vice President of Sales, 1993-1995
Director, Sales Department, 1990-1993

SAS Airlines, Los Angeles, CA
Regional Sales Manager, 1985-1990
District Sales Manager, 1981-1985
Sales Representative, 1978-1981

                                        Page 1 of 2

STEVEN TYLER - 2

EDUCATION

<u>Colorado University</u>, Denver, CO
M.B.A., June 1978

<u>Rivers College</u>, Beaver Falls, KY
B.S. in Communications, June 1976

SEMINARS

<u>Sponsored by Pacific Marketing Institute</u>
International Sales and Marketing
Domestic Sales and Marketing
Management and Administration
Travel Sales Incentives
Telemarketing

REFERENCES

Available on request

HARRIET SCHUMACHER

1414 N. Montebello Drive
Berkeley, CA 98028
415/555-4930

EDUCATION: <u>University of California at Berkeley</u>
                    Bachelor of Science in Marketing
                    Expected June 1998

HONORS: Beta Gamma Epsilon Society
                    Dean's List
                    Manley Writing Award, 1996

ACTIVITIES: Treasurer, Gamma Gamma Gamma Sorority
                    Freshman Advisor
                    Homecoming Planning Committee
                    Alumni Welcoming Committee

WORK
EXPERIENCE: <u>AT&T</u>, New York, NY
                    Marketing Intern, 1997
                    Assisted marketing staff in the areas of research,
                    demographics, sales forecasts, identifying new
                    customers, and developing special promotions.

                    <u>University of California at Berkeley</u>
                    Office Assistant, Journalism School, 1995-1997
                    Assisted with student registration, filing, and
                    data entry. Arranged application materials.
                    Assembled course packs.

SKILLS: Fluent in German. Hands-on computer experience
                    using Lotus 1-2-3 and dBASE III.

REFERENCES: On request.

PATRICK H. McCOY
1701 N. Hampshire Rd.
Miami, FL 03908
305/555-3909 (Home)
McCOY@Newmark.org (E-Mail)

OBJECTIVE: A position as sales manager for a mid-size manufacturer.

WORK
EXPERIENCE: NEWMARK INDUSTRIES, Miami, FL
Account Executive, 1997 to present

Manage sales accounts in south Florida territory for consumer electronics company. Expanded customer base by 28% during the last two years. Collaborate with marketing department to develop direct-mail campaigns. Maintain accounts through daily phone contact and frequent on-site visits. Train new hires.

POTISCO, Terre Haute, IN
Sales Representative, 1993 to 1997

Handled sales to customers, particularly contractors. Priced bid estimates as required. Oversaw customer and public relations that helped to build the company's image. Set up office procedures where necessary.

HONOCO, INC., Chicago, IL
Sales Representative, 1990 to 1993

Developed and managed new territories. Built sales through cold calls on physicians, hospitals, retailers, and wholesalers. Researched competitive product lines. Developed effective promotions and sales incentives.

EDUCATION: WHEATON COLLEGE, Wheaton, IL
B.A. in Business, 1990

SEMINARS: Sales and Marketing Institute Courses in the following
*Sales and Marketing for the Nineties
*Marketing Strategies for Manufacturers

REFERENCES: Available on request.

WILLIAM ROBERT GARRETT
5050 W. Palatine Road
Palatine, IL 60067
847/555-3789 (Home)
847/555-1000 (Work)

JOB OBJECTIVE

A management-level position in computer sales where I can utilize my sales and technical experience in the computer industry.

EXPERIENCE

Sales

- Handled sales accounts for northwest suburban Chicago area.
- Expanded customer base by 25% during my tenure.
- Conducted field visits to solve customers' problems.
- Maintained daily contact with customers to ensure good customer relations.
- Developed product information guides and sales manuals.

Technical

- Installed and maintained operating systems.
- Defined and oversaw network lists and tables.
- Coordinated problem solving with phone companies.
- Performance tuned subsystems and networks.
- Planned and installed new hardware and software.

Systems Analysis

- Documented procedures for mechanization of payroll department.
- Created standards and procedures for main accounting system.
- Coordinated requirements for new delivery system with production department.
- Developed test procedures for verification of new application.
- Developed distribution lists, user IDs, and standards for electronic mail system.

EMPLOYMENT HISTORY

MICROTECH COMPUTERS, Northbrook, IL
Account Executive, 1989-Present

APPLE COMPUTERS, Berkeley, CA
Technical Support Specialist, 1982-1989

DATALOG INC., St. Louis, MO
Systems Analyst, 1971-1981

Page 1 of 2

William Robert Garrett - 2

EDUCATION

UNIVERSITY OF CHICAGO, Hyde Park, IL
M.S. in Mathematics, 1970
Graduated with Honors

NORTHWESTERN UNIVERSITY, Evanston, IL
B.S. in Communications, June 1967

PROFESSIONAL AFFILIATIONS

Computer Sales Association
Illinois Business Council
Citizens for a Cleaner Environment

SEMINARS

Microtech Sales Seminars
Apple Technical Workshops

REFERENCES AVAILABLE ON REQUEST

DONALD R. CRUMP

5001 Providence Street   **201/555-8000**
Washington, DC 02930   **201/555-3894**

Objective: A position as marketing manager for Graphics, Inc.

Experience: BURGER WORLD, INC., Washington, DC
Marketing Director, 1993 - Present
Develop successful marketing campaigns for fast food chain. Initiated
and currently maintain positive working relationship with radio, T.V.,
and print media. Implement marketing strategies to increase sales at
less profitable outlets. Designed and manage a training program for
sales managers and staff.

HI FIDELITY STEREO COMPANY, Newark, NJ
Marketing Representative, 1988 - 1993
Demonstrated electronic equipment in stereo and department stores.
Analyzed and reported customer reactions to manufacturers. Designed
fliers and advertising to promote products. Made frequent calls to
retail outlets.

INTERCO, New York, NY
Sales Representative, 1981 - 1988
Identified clients' needs and problems and provided personalized
solutions. Resolved service and billing problems. Delivered sales
presentations. Identified potential customers and established new
accounts.

Education: GEORGETOWN UNIVERSITY, Washington, D.C.
B.S. in Marketing, 1981

NEW YORK COLLEGE OF BUSINESS
Various marketing seminars, 1982 - 1984

Skills: Fluent in Spanish.
Knowledge of WordPerfect, Excel, and Lotus 1-2-3.

REFERENCES AVAILABLE

MATTHEW R. CLARKSON

1251 S. Maple Ave.
Des Moines, IA 52909
515/555-4999 (Day)
515/555-3429 (Evening)

OBJECTIVE: Manager of the hardware department of a major department store.

ACHIEVEMENTS: *Promoted from customer service representative to salesperson and then to assistant manager in hardware at Sears in Des Moines.

*Managed a staff of six, including hiring, job training, and supervision.

*Helped to reorganize inventory control methods.

*Assisted customers in choosing and using hardware products.

*Combined managerial and sales talents to increase department sales.

WORK HISTORY: SEARS, Des Moines, IA

Assistant Manager	3/98 to Present
Salesperson	2/96 to 3/98
Customer Service Representative	8/95 to 2/96

SAM'S HARDWARE, West Petersville, IA

Stock Clerk	Summers, 1993 to 1995

EDUCATION: Des Moines Township High School, Des Moines, IA
Graduated June 1985
Top 25% of class
Student Council Secretary
Homecoming Committee

Redbrook College, Des Moines, IA
Various night courses, including Retail Sales Management and Supervisory Techniques.

REFERENCES: On request.

GLORIA GARLAND

1220 Market St. #3, San Francisco, CA 92290
415/555-5508

OBJECTIVE: A management-level position in the publishing industry.

**WORK
EXPERIENCE:**

BAY MAGAZINE, San Francisco, CA
Regional Manager, 1997 - present
Oversee administration, negotiation, and maintenance of exchange agreements and sales promotion. Track market changes, with responsibility for executing responses to developments. Recently led magazine's Eastern edition through a reorganization period. Planned and implemented new editions in the South.

SANDLER IMPORTS, Sausalito, CA
Sales Coordinator, 1993 - 1997
Managed ten field representatives. Handled information dissemination and distribution. Codesigned a full-color catalog. Placed advertising in major trade publications. Promoted products at trade shows. Maintained inventory status reports and personnel records.

REDWOOD PUBLISHING CO., San Francisco, CA
Distribution Assistant, 1988 - 1993
Developed new distribution outlets through cold calls and follow-up visits. Increased distribution in my district by 45% over a three-year period. Coordinated a direct mail program that increased magazine subscriptions 120%.

XEROX CO., Atlanta, CA
Sales Representative, 1985 - 1988
Sold and serviced office copiers to businesses and schools in the greater Atlanta area. Maintained good customer relations through frequent calls and visits. Identified potential customers.

EDUCATION:

Miami University, Miami, OH
B.S. in Communications, 1985

Page 1 of 2

GLORIA GARLAND - Page 2

PROFESSIONAL **MEMBERSHIPS:**	National Association of Importers Sausalito Community Association San Francisco Chamber of Commerce American Publishing Association
SEMINARS:	"Publishing in the '90s," Chicago, IL "International Publishing," New York, NY
REFERENCES:	Available on request.

Sally Johnson
3240 Santa Monica Blvd.
Los Angeles, CA 90028
213-555-9832

Objective

A position as an assistant sales manager for an automobile manufacturer.

Skills and Accomplishments

Sales
- *Identified clients' needs and problems and provided solutions*
- *Explained billing policies and resolved problems with outstanding accounts*
- *Created and delivered sales presentations*
- *Conducted market research and established new accounts*
- *Increased client base by 40%*

Development
- *Researched competitive product lines and drafted reports to District Manager*
- *Prepared sales forecasts and sales goals reports*
- *Developed monthly sales plans for maintaining accounts and resolving potential problems*

Employment History

Yugo America, Inc., Los Angeles, CA
Sales Representative, 1/98 to Present

Track Autoparts, Inc., Burbank, CA
Sales Representative, 9/95 to 2/97

Apple One Temporary, Glendale, CA
Sales Representative, 5/94 to 9/95

Education

Burbank College of Art, Burbank, CA
B.A. in Art, 1994

References

Available on request.

THEODORE WELLINGTON
34 Washington Drive
New York, NY 10019
212/555-4904

JOB OBJECTIVE

A senior management position in sales and marketing.

ACHIEVEMENTS

- Introduced new and existing product lines through presentations to marketing directors.
- Developed new product that resulted in increased sales.
- Increased sales from $3 million to $12 million during the past six years.
- Supervised five sales agencies throughout the United States and Canada.
- Developed fifteen new accounts.
- Researched the market in order to coordinate product line with current trends.
- Increased company's share of the market through improved quality products.

EMPLOYMENT HISTORY

Surf City Skateboard Company, New York, NY
Vice President of Sales and Marketing, 1989 - Present

Nike, Inc., San Bernadino, CA
Sales and Marketing Manager, 1984 - 1989

Vons Ltd., Los Angeles, CA
Sales Representative, 1979 - 1984

EDUCATION

University of Southern California, Los Angeles, CA
B.S. in Marketing, 1968

SEMINARS

Manhattan Sales and Marketing Seminar, 1997, 1998
National Marketing Association Conference, 1992 - 1996

REFERENCES

Provided on request.

YOSHEMA MUNO

7640 N. Redden Road
Skokie, IL 60076
847/555-3908
847/555-2300

JOB OBJECTIVE

A position as manager of a store that sells quality shoes and accessories.

EXPERIENCE

Florsheim Shoes, Skokie, IL
Assistant Manager, 1997 to Present

Serve as assistant manager of a quality shoe store. Partially responsible for supervision of eight salespeople. Research customers' buying habits and preferences. Handle promotion and mailings for special sales and in-store events. Increase sales through personal attention to customer needs.

Handleman Shoe Store, Lincolnwood, IL
Salesperson, 1993 to 1997

Sold high-quality women's shoes at an exclusive store. Named top salesperson of 1996 and 1997. Maintained a clean, attractive store area and organized inventory.

Florsheim Shoes, Chicago, IL
Salesperson, 1990 to 1993

Sold shoes. Assisted customers in making purchase decisions. Organized and maintained stock and delivery. Helped with window displays.

EDUCATION

Stevenson Community College, Chicago, IL
Attended two years. Majored in business.

Calumet High School, Calumet, IL
Graduated 1990. Won Science Award.

REFERENCES

Available on request.

DAREN TREVOL
43433 N. Melrose Ave.
Elmhurst, IL 60189
847/555-4328

OBJECTIVE:	Senior Vice-President of Sales and Marketing for Vincent Electronics Inc.
ACHIEVEMENTS:	Marketing

* Researched computer market to coordinate product line with current tastes and buying trends.
* Developed new approaches to marketing software products, including in-store displays and advertising.
* Organized and planned convention displays and strategies.

Sales

* Introduced new and existing product lines through presentations to major clients.
* Increased sales from $27 million to $50 million in five years.
* Initiated and developed nine new accounts.
* Supervised five sales agencies nationwide.

WORK HISTORY:	Vincent Electronics, Inc., Elmhurst, IL Sales and Marketing Manager, 1995 to Present Porcelana Inc., Melrose Park, IL Product Coordinator, 1990 to 1995 Radio Shack, Inc., New York, NY Sales Representative, 1985 to 1990
EDUCATION:	New York University, New York, NY B.S. 1995 Major: Business Administration Minor: Computer Science
REFERENCES:	Available on request

JOHN L. RYDER

211 W. Fourth Street #211
Brooklyn, NY 10001
847/555-9080

JOB OBJECTIVE

Seeking a sales management position in a medium to large-sized insurance company.

ACCOMPLISHMENTS

Increased sales 17% the first year I sold group policies to businesses and unions. Sales increases have averaged 15% to 20% in subsequent years.

Chaired a committee that developed a sales manual that explained group insurance sales techniques.

Served as insurance adjustor for Brooklyn Health Company, a 20,000-member HMO.

Handled highly technical reimbursements by the state to the HMO.

Wrote and edited annual reports and quarterly reports.

Investigated and reported on adjustments and claims.

WORK EXPERIENCE

Interco Insurance Company, New York, NY
Insurance Agent, 1995 - Present

Brooklyn Health Company, Brooklyn, NY
Health Insurance Adjustor, 1990 - 1995

City of St. Louis, St. Louis, MO
Claims Adjustor, 1985 - 1990

EDUCATION

M.B.A., Washington University, St. Louis, MO, 1984
B.A., Washington University, St. Louis, MO, 1982

OTHER

Extensive experience with QuarkXPress, Microsoft Word, and Excel

Willing to travel and to relocate if necessary

JAMES BROWN
12 Hinman Avenue
St. Paul, MN 51111
612/555-6490
612/555-6565

JOB OBJECTIVE

A position as a marketing representative for a manufacturer of textiles.

PROFESSIONAL ACHIEVEMENTS

Marketing

* Demonstrated the value of quantity purchases to customers.
* Researched industry competition to refine selling techniques.
* Projected success of new products through surveys and questionnaires.

Sales

* Established and maintained an excellent relationship with over 100 accounts
  in the textile industry.
* Resolved customer complaints promptly.
* Provided customers with detailed information on product line.
* Named Salesperson of the Month six times.

WORK HISTORY

Rand Textiles, Inc., St. Paul, MN
Sales Representative, 4/97-Present

St. Paul Woolen Products, St. Paul, MN
Salesperson, 5/94-3/97

EDUCATION

Potterville Community College, Pottersville, MN
1992-1994

St. Rose High School, St. Olaf, MN
Graduated June, 1992

REFERENCES

Available upon request.

SCOTT JONES

16 E. Mayfair Road
Arlington Heights, IL 60005
312/555-6721 (Day)
312/555-9339 (Evening)

OBJECTIVE: A sales position in commercial real estate.

EXPERIENCE: ERA Realty, Inc., Arlington Heights, IL
Domestic Real Estate Salesperson, 3/97 to Present
Sell homes in the Northwest suburban area. Interact with clients,
real estate agents, brokers, and bank personnel. Awarded ERA
Northwest Suburban Salesperson of the Year, 1998.

Arlington Heights Camera Shop, Arlington Heights, IL
Camera Salesperson, 1992 to 1997
Sold cameras and film. Assisted customers in filling orders and
making repairs. Trained new members of sales staff. Reorganized
inventory system.

ACTIVITIES: Member, Northwest Suburban Realty Association, 1997 to Present

Member, Arlington Heights Chamber of Commerce

EDUCATION: University of Illinois at Chicago, 1994 - 1996
Major: Business

Harper Community College, Palatine, IL, 1993 - 1994

SKILLS: Proficient in WordPerfect 6.1 and Lotus 1-2-3

REFERENCES: Provided upon request.

<u>SANDRA L. PEARSON</u>

12 E. Tenth Street
San Francisco, CA 94890
415/555-2343

<u>JOB OBJECTIVE</u>

A management position in cable television advertising sales.

<u>EXPERIENCE</u>

- Sold space in television for four major clients in the automotive industry.
- Served as a liaison between clients and television and radio station salespeople.
- Researched demographic and public buying habits for clients.
- Sold space for daytime programming on local TV station.
- Advised station on content and suitability of ads.
- Served as a liaison between station and those purchasing advertising space.

<u>EMPLOYMENT HISTORY</u>

Medialink Advertising Agency, San Francisco, CA
Television Space Sales, September 1995 - Present

KTUT Television, Portland, OR
Television Space Sales, October 1993 - August 1995

KFTF Radio, Berkeley, CA
Staff Sales Assistant, June 1991 - June 1993

<u>EDUCATION</u>

B.A. in Communications, University of California at Berkeley, 1993

<u>HONORS</u>

Seeger Award, Outstanding Communications Senior, 1993
Dean's List, five semesters
Salutatorian, Overland High School, Palo Alto, CA 1989

REFERENCES ON REQUEST

MARTIN T. CHRISTENSON

65 W. Harrison
Minneapolis, MN 44490
612/555-1212 (DAY)
612/555-2901 (EVENING)

JOB OBJECTIVE

Sales manager for a computer software manufacturer.

PROFESSIONAL EXPERIENCE

Sales and Promotion

- Made cold calls and visits to software retailers that resulted in increased accounts.
- Visited and serviced existing accounts to encourage continued sales.
- Advised customers on options available to meet a wide range of product needs.
- Handled dealer requests for information and sample products.

Marketing

- Researched competitive products to evaluate competitors' strengths and weaknesses.
- Planned a marketing strategy that resulted in 20% increase in accounts.
- Maintained demographic data in order to ascertain buyer profile.

EMPLOYMENT HISTORY

Thomas Software Inc., Minneapolis, MN
Assistant Sales Manager 1995 - Present
Sales Representative, 1993 - 1995

Quaker & Company, St. Paul, MN
Marketing Assistant, 1992 - 1993

USA Computer Sales, Skokie, IL
Salesperson, 1990 - 1992

Bennigan's Restaurant, Columbus, OH
Waiter, 1989 - 1990

Page 1 of 2

MARTIN T. CHRISTENSON - 2

EDUCATION

Washington University, St. Louis, MO
B.A. in Marketing, 1992

HONORS

Phi Beta Kappa, 1992
Dean's List, 1990 - 1992
Terrance C. Maples Marketing Scholarship Recipient, 1990 - 1991
President, Student Activities Board, 1992

SPECIAL SKILLS

Knowledge of WordPerfect 6.1, Microsoft Works, PowerPoint, and Excel

REFERENCES

Provided on request.

CHRISTOPHER POLLEN
8909 S. Alvira Street
Los Angeles, CA 90028

904/555-9090

OBJECTIVE

To obtain a position in market research where I can focus
on needs/trends analysis, demographics, and market surveys.

WORK EXPERIENCE

SOUTHERN CALIFORNIA TOURS, INC., Los Angeles, CA
RESEARCH ANALYST ASSISTANT, 1997 to Present
Project sales potential by interpreting sales figures from
yearly data. Develop target campaigns that increase the
efficiency of company's direct mail approach. Analyze incoming market data on customers for demographic purposes.
Initiate changes in marketing strategy that improve
customer satisfaction.

AMERICAN HOSPITAL SUPPLY CORPORATION, Evanston, IL
SALES ASSISTANT, 1993 to 1997
Researched and wrote training bulletins on communication and
sales strategy for the sales staff. Trained new salespeople.
Prepared proposals for the regional sales manager. Handled
scheduling and travel arrangements for the sales department.

EDUCATION

NORTHWESTERN UNIVERSITY, Evanston, IL
B.A. in English, 1993

HONORS

Graduated with honors in English, 1993
Dean's List, 1992, 1993

ACTIVITIES

President, Senior Writing Club, 1993
Captain, Men's Tennis Team, 1992 - 1993

SPECIAL SKILLS

Working knowledge of French and German
Lotus 1-2-3, Microsoft Works

References Available

JANE T. HERNANDEZ
5555 Euclid Avenue
Ft. Lauderdale, FL 33053
305/555-8982 (Day)
305/555-6001 (Evening)

OBJECTIVE: A sales management position with a machine tool manufacturer where I can apply my abilities and experience in sales and marketing.

WORK
EXPERIENCE: **Florida Hydraulics, Inc., Miami, FL**
Assistant Sales Manager, January 1995 - Present
Manage a staff of seven sales representatives. Supervise the production of a marketing newsletter that has circulation throughout the company. Co-write the annual marketing plan. Serve as a liaison between sales staff and upper management.

Peaston Machine Tools, Inc., Tampa, FL
Sales Representative, March 1992 - November 1994
Sold machine tools to business and industry. Wrote articles on sales techniques for monthly newsletter. Handled seven accounts in which sales rose 29% during my tenure.

EDUCATION: B.S. in Civil Engineering
Miami University, Miami, FL
August 1991

AFFILIATIONS: Society of Civil Engineers, New York, NY
1993 - Present

Machine Tools Sales Organization, Chicago, IL
1994 - Present

SKILLS: Fluent in Spanish and French

REFERENCES: Available on request

CAROL A. BADEN

Permanent Address:
South East Hollow Road
Berlin, NY 10951
(518) 555-6057

Temporary Address:
150 Fort Washington Avenue
New York, NY 10032
(212) 555-4959

OBJECTIVE: A sales trainee position with a financial planning group.

EDUCATION: Bachelor of Science, Communications
Minor: Economics
New York University, New York, NY
Date of Graduation: May 1998
Communications G.P.A. 3.6
Academic G.P.A. 3.5

EXPERIENCE: V.I.T.A. (Volunteer Income Tax Assistance), Spring 1997
Provided income tax assistance to lower income and
elderly taxpayers who were unable to prepare returns or pay for
professional assistance.

Tutor, Economics Department, New York, University, 1997
Helped students to better understand basic concepts in
the study of economics.

Salesperson, Parkersons Department Store, Brooklyn, NY,
Summer, 1995
Assisted customers with purchases; responsible for cash
management, inventory, and displays.

Clerical Assistant, Order Department, Castle Catering,
Brooklyn, NY
Took phone orders; assisted with bookkeeping.

HONORS: Senior Service Award, New York University, 1997
Dean's List, Fall 1995 and Spring 1997

REFERENCES: Available upon request.

JASMINE TOPPER
5 E. Randall Road
Providence, RI 00898
401/555-6768

GOAL: Assistant Sales Manager

WORK
HISTORY:
<u>American Telecom</u>, Providence, RI
Sales Representative, 1993 - Present
Identify customer needs and problems and provide personalized
Identify potential new customers and establish new accounts.
Increased client base by 30% during tenure. Prepare sales
forecasts and sales reports.

<u>Amadala Foods, Inc.</u>, Boston, MA
Sales Representative, 1990 - 1993
Orchestrated market analyses and researched competition
for reports to the district manager. Developed monthly sales
plans that identified necessary account maintenance and
specific problems that required attention. Resolved service and
billing problems. Maintained daily sales logs and referral logs.

<u>Century 21 Realty</u>, Cambridge, MA
Salesperson, 1985 - 1990
Sold homes in the Cambridge area. Interacted with clients, real
estate agents, brokers, and bank personnel. Awarded Salesperson
of the Year award three times.

EDUCATION: B.A. in Business, 1984
Cambridge College, Cambridge, MA
Received Harriet Johnson Business Scholarship

SKILLS: Proficient in WordPerfect 6.1 and Lotus 1-2-3

REFERENCES AVAILABLE

QUENTIN PORLEAN
12 Derbyshire Drive
East St. Louis, IL 60989

314/555-8932

JOB SOUGHT

A position as manager of the electronics department of a major department store.

WORK EXPERIENCE

<u>Bergstrom's</u>, St. Louis, MO

Assistant Manager 1994 - Present
Salesperson, 1992 - 1994
<u>Customer Service Representative, 1991 - 1992</u>
   Promoted from customer service representative to salesperson and then to assistant manager of electronics at Bergstrom's. Currently manage a staff of four. Responsible for hiring, job training, and supervision. Oversee inventory control. Assist customers in choosing electronic products and designing entertainment centers.

<u>Radio Shack</u>, East St. Louis, IL

<u>Salesperson, Summers, 1989 -1991</u>
   Sold electronic products and equipment. Handled inventory and product orders. Assisted customers with technical questions.

EDUCATION

<u>East St. Louis High School</u>, East St. Louis, IL
   Graduated June 1991
   Top 10 percent of class
   Student Council President
   Member, Black Students' Alliance

<u>Barton Community College</u>, St. Louis, MO
   Attended, 1991
   Courses included Sales Techniques and Retail Management

REFERENCES

Provided on request

GINA STEVENSON
433 Maple Drive
Hoffman Estates, IL 60035
847/555-2341

OBJECTIVE

To become part of the sales and marketing team at Laura Ashley, Inc.

WORK EXPERIENCE

Gina Designs, Hoffman Estates, IL
Owner/Designer, 1991 to Present

Established a national market for my original clothing line. Display and merchandise clothing items at retail stores and fashion shows. Increased sales 300% in the past two years. Order supplies; process purchase orders and invoices. Ship and deliver product.

Talbot's Inc., Schaumburg, IL
Assistant Sales Manager, 1990 to 1991

Sell clothing and gifts at the retail level. Order stock and maintain inventory. Increased sales by developing in-store promotion program.

Lynn's Hallmark, Arlington Heights, IL
Manager, 1985 to 1990
Salesperson, 1980 to 1985

Managed gift shop and supervised ten employees. Maintained inventory, sales records, and bank deposits. Ordered products; processed purchase orders and invoices. Handled all payroll duties. Sold gift items.

EDUCATION

B.A., Interior design, Wheaton College, Wheaton, IL 1990

REFERENCES

Provided on request.

JAMES KENDALL
509 27th Street #4556
New York, NY 10019

212-555-0909
212-555-0900 (Fax)

EXPERIENCE:

JONES & JONES, New York, NY
Commodity Broker, 1993 to Present
- Handle more than 500 clients as a specialist in corn and wheat futures.
- Provide written market forecasts to salespeople.
- Publish and distribute a weekly newsletter on futures.

KAREN SCHWARTZ, Inc., New York, NY
Commodity Sales, 1990 to 1993
- Managed a client list of more than 300.
- Researched and wrote in-house reports on wheat market forecasts.
- Named Salesperson of the Year, 1995.

PICKERING, PICKERING & GOLD, Chicago, IL
Commodity Trader, 1985 to 1990
- Traded cattle futures in-pit on the Chicago Commodities Exchange.

EDUCATION:

B.A., Brown University, 1985
Major: Economics
Minor: English

PROFESSIONAL MEMBERSHIPS:

American Society of Commodities Brokers
New York Business Alliance

SEMINARS:

"Commodity Futures," University of Wisconsin, Madison, 1994

REFERENCES AVAILABLE

JOANNA P. DOBSON
5660 W. Seventh Street
Des Moines, IA 50399
600-555-3453 (Day)
600-359-9000 (Evening)

OBJECTIVE:

To be placed in a marketing research position where I can assist in the development of sales and marketing strategies for a major medical supplies company.

ACHIEVEMENTS:

Developed and implemented marketing strategies for a major manufacturer of disposable medical supplies sold for the purposes of anesthesia administration, IV therapy, and open-heart surgery.

Served as a research and development specialist for a surgical supply manufacturer.

Managed a five-state sales area on the East Coast. Increased sales 38% during my three-year tenure as a surgical supplies sales representative. Increased number of clients by 27%, which led to a significant increase in revenue.

WORK EXPERIENCE:

Americon, Inc., Des Moines, IA
Marketing Assistant, 1997 to Present

Meico Surgical Company, Carbondale, IL
Research and Development Assistant, 1995 to 1997

US Medical, Harrisburg, PA
Sales Representative, 1993 to 1995

EDUCATION:

B.S., Biology, University of Pennsylvania, 1993
Graduated in top 10% of class

REFERENCES:

Available on request

IVOR T. KOPESKI

501 W. Glendale Blvd.   Kansas City, MO 51132   816/555-9090

Objective

Regional sales manager for a national pharmaceutical manufacturer/distributor.

Experience

RFB Pharmaceuticals, Kansas City, MO
District Sales Manager, 1994-Present
Direct the selling and servicing of accounts to physicians, pharmacies, and hospitals in the Kansas City area. Increased sales by 50% during the last four years. Initiated an incentive plan that resulted in 21 new accounts. Worked with production department to improve product quality.

Jacobs & Jacobs Advertising, Trenton, NJ
Display Coordinator, 1991-1994
Coordinated and supervised the installation of displays in men's clothing stores in the Trenton area. Managed a five-person office in all aspects of display planning and production. Worked to help place the firm in the syndicated display advertising field.

Mark Shale, Inc., Schaumburg, IL
Retail Store Manager, 1987-1991
Promoted from salesperson to assistant manager to manager within two years. Supervised the designing of display for interior and windows. Handled all aspects of personnel, sales promotions, inventory control, and new product.   Interacted with corporate management frequently.

Education

Harper College, Palatine, IL
Attended 1985-1987
Majored in Advertising

American Institute, Putnum, NJ
Completed course on sales techniques, 1993

Page 1 of 2

Ivor T. Kopeski
-2-

Memberships

American Display Advertisers, 1991-1994
Treasurer, 1992

Kansas City Sales Association
Member, 1994 to Present

Kansas City Community Development Association
Member, 1994 to Present
Co-chair, Community Fundraising Project

Awards

Salesperson of the Year
Mark Shale Corporation
1991

Excellence in Advertising Award
American Display Advertisers
1993

Community Service Certificate
Kansas City Chamber of Commerce
1997

References

On request

GERALD ROBERT SCAMPI

4890 W. 57th Street
New York, NY 10019
212/555-3678

JOB OBJECTIVE

Vice President of promotion for a communications company.

PROFESSIONAL EXPERIENCE

1996-Present   ATLANTIC RECORDS, New York, NY
Promotion Manager.
Develop and execute all marketing strategies for record promotion in New York, New Jersey, and Massachusetts. Interface with sales department and retail stores to ensure adequate product placement. Attend various company-sponsored sales, marketing, and management seminars.

1987-1996   RSO RECORDS, Miami, FL
Promotion Manager.
Planned all marketing strategies for record promotions in the southeast United States. Worked closely with sales and touring bands to ensure product visibility in the marketplace.

1985-1987   WCFL RADIO, Chicago, IL
On-Air Personality.
Played CHR music. Made TV appearances and public events appearances for the station. Organized and staffed station's news department. Promoted to Music Director after one year.

1980-1985   WGLT RADIO, Atlanta, GA
Program Director, Music Director, and News Director

EDUCATION

COLUMBIA COLLEGE, Chicago, IL
Attended 1979-1980
Studied Audio Engineering

REFERENCES AVAILABLE

JIM HORNFELD
1800 W. Third Street
San Francisco, CA 98088
415/555-9202

OBJECTIVE:

A management position in sales and marketing.

PROFESSIONAL EXPERIENCE:

Rolex Watches, Inc., San Francisco, CA
Vice President of Sales and Marketing, 1989-Present
Increased watch sales from $3 million to $12 million during the past six years. Introduced new and existing product lines through presentation to marketing directors and manufacturers throughout the United States and Canada. Developed new products expanding from watches to other accessories, which resulted in increased sales. Researched watch market to coordinate product line with current fashion trends. Increased company's share of the market through improved quality products.

Peters and Company, Salt Lake City, UT
District Sales Manager, 1984-1989
Planned successful strategies to identify and develop new accounts. Increased sales by at least 25 percent each year. Researched and analyzed market conditions in order to expand customer base. Developed weekly and monthly sales goals and strategies. Supervised seven sales representatives.

Herzz, Inc., Los Angeles, CA
Sales Representative, 1979-1984
Developed and managed new territories. Built sales through calls on retailers and whole-salers. Developed creative techniques for increasing product sales. Maintained current knowledge of competitive products. Wrote weekly and monthly sales reports.

EDUCATION:

University of Southern California, Los Angeles, CA
B.S. in Marketing, 1978

SEMINARS:

Southern California Marketing Seminar, 1997 and 1998
National Retailers Association, 1992 - 1996

REFERENCES:

Available on request.

DAVID P. JENKINS
36 N. Coldwater Canyon
North Hollywood, CA 90390
818/555-3472

JOB OBJECTIVE:

A position as a sales/marketing manager where I can utilize my knowledge and experience by combining high volume selling of major accounts with an administrative ability that increases sales through encouragement of sales team.

EMPLOYMENT
HISTORY:

TRIBOR INDUSTRIES, Los Angeles, CA
Regional Sales Manager, 1995-Present

Manage sales of all product lines in western markets for a leading maker of fine linens. Represent four corporate divisions with combined annual sales of approximately $3 million. Direct and motivate a sales force of twelve in planned selling to achieve company goals.

TRIBOR INDUSTRIES, Los Angeles, CA
District Manager, 1990-1995

Acted as district sales manager for the Los Angeles metropolitan area. Built wholesale and dealer distribution substantially over a five-year period, culminating in promotion to regional sales manager.

AMERICAN OFFICE SUPPLY, Chicago, IL
Assistant to Sales Manager, 1986-1990

Handled both internal and external areas of sales and marketing, including samples, advertising, and pricing. Served as company sales representative and sold a variety of office supplies to retail outlets.

EDUCATION:

University of Michigan, Ann Arbor, MI
B.A. in Business Administration
Major: Management

Page 1 of 2

David P. Jenkins   -2-

SEMINARS: National Management Association Seminar, 1994
                    "Sales Strategies 2000"

                    Los Angeles Business Institute Seminars, 1993-1998
                    "Motivating Experienced Sales Staff"
                    "Advanced Direct Marketing Techniques"

HONORS: Manager of the Year
                    Tribor Industries, 1997

                    Top Monthly Sales, five times
                    American Office Supply, 1986-1990

REFERENCES: Provided upon request

CHRISTOPHER BERNARD SMALLS
600 W. Porter Street, # 5
Las Vegas, NV 89890
514/555-3893

OBJECTIVE

A position as a marketing trainee in a manufacturing company.

EDUCATION

University of Nevada, Las Vegas, NV
Bachelor of Science in Business
Expected June 1998

HONORS

Dean's List for four semesters
Dornburn Scholarship
University of Nevada, Las Vegas,
 Undergraduate Business Award

WORK EXPERIENCE

Porter Rand & Associates, Seattle, WA
Sales Intern, 1997
Assisted sales staff in the areas of research, demographics, sales forecasts, identifying new customers, and promotion.

University of Nevada, Las Vegas, NV
Research/Office Assistant, 1995-1996
Researched and compiled materials for department professors. Arranged filing system and supervisor's library. Organized department inventory.

SPECIAL SKILLS

Experience using IBM and Apple hardware and WordPerfect 6.0 and dBASE III software programs.

SARA STEVENS
332 E. Geobert Road
Terre Haute, IN 48930
317/555-3890

Goal:	Manager of a florist shop.
Work History:	
1994-Present	**Terry's Flowers, Terre Haute, IN** **Assistant Sales Manager** Sell flowers, wait on customers, fill phone orders, handle special orders, and design window displays. Place ads for special promotions. Represent store at sales conventions.
1993-1994	**Avant Books, Indianapolis, IN** **Salesperson** Sold books to customers, filled special orders, and arranged inventory. Handled customer returns and special requests.
Education:	Revers High School, Indianapolis, IN Graduated June 1993 Ranked 15 in class of 250 Worked in student bookstore for four years.
References:	Available on request

EUNICE T. BODEANE
1221 E. Cambridge Avenue
Lynn, MA 02129

617/555-8800

OBJECTIVE: A position as publicist with an arts organization.

WORK HISTORY: **Boston Opera Company, Boston, MA**
Public Relations Assistant, 1996-Present
Compose press releases and public service announcements
that publicize opera events. Develop contacts with Boston
entertainment columnists that result in extensive coverage.
Maintain calendar of advertising deadlines. Write ad copy
for print and radio.

Sandra Watt Agency, Boston, MA
Editorial/Public Relations Assistant, 1995-1996
Edited technical and literary manuscripts. Compiled a directory
of Boston editors and publishers for agency use. Organized an
educational workshop for local writers.

EDUCATION: **Ithaca University, Ithaca, New York**
B.S. in Advertising, June 1996

Courses: Marketing Techniques, Advertising, Corporate Public
Relations, P.R. Techniques.

HONORS: Sigma Kappa Nu Honorary Society
Honors in Advertising
Dean's List
Myron T. Kapp Public Relations Award

ACTIVITIES: Student Government Representative
Homecoming Committee
Soccer Club

REFERENCES: Provided on request.

ALLISON SPRINGS
15 Hilton House
Colorado Women's College
Denver, CO 80220
303/555-2550

Job Sought:

Position within a government or nonprofit agency that can benefit from
my organizational and marketing skills.

Skills and Experience:

Negotiating Skills:

Developed negotiating skills through participation in student government
that enabled me to persuade others of the advantages of compromise.

Promotional Skills:

Contributed greatly to my successful campaign for class office
(Junior Class Vice President) through the effective use of posters, displays,
and other visual aids. Participated in committee projects and fund-raising efforts
that netted $15,000 for the junior class project.

People Skills:

As Junior Class Vice President, balanced the concerns of different groups
in order to reach a common goal. As a claims interviewer with a state public
assistance agency, dealt with people under stressful circumstances. As a research
assistant with a law firm, interacted with both lawyers and clerical workers.
As a lifeguard, learned how to manage groups.

Education:

Colorado Women's College
Bachelor of Arts in Political Science
Degree expected June 1998
Vice President Junior Class
Student Council
Harvest Committee

Work Experience:

McCall, McCrow & McCoy, Westrow, CO
Research Assistant, January 1996 to present

Department of Public Assistance, Denver, CO
Claims Interviewer, September 1995 - December 1995

Shilo Pool, Shilo, NE
Lifeguard, 1991 - 1994

References:

Provided on request

Caroline A. Carolson

15001 Irvine Meadows Drive
Calistoga, FL 28088
305/555-8398

OBJECTIVE:	A management-level sales position.
EMPLOYMENT HISTORY:	

Simpco, Inc., Tampa, FL
Regional Sales Manager, 1993 to Present
Manage sales of all product lines in southern markets for a leading manufacturer of fixtures. Represent five corporate divisions of the company, with sales in excess of $2 million annually. Direct and motivate a sales force of 12 in planned selling to achieve company goals.

Lucky Industries, Miami, FL
District Manager, 1988 to 1993
Acted as sales representative for the Miami metropolitan area. Built both wholesales and dealer distribution substantially during my tenure. Developed monthly sales plans that identified necessary account maintenance and specific problems that required attention.

National Office Products, Inc., Baton Rouge, LA
Assistant Sales Manager, 1979 to 1988
Handled both internal and external areas of sales and marketing, including samples, advertising, and pricing. Served as company sales representative and sold a variety of office supplies to retail stores.

EDUCATION:	Smith College, Omaha, NE B.A. in English, 1977
SEMINARS:	American Sales Association Seminars, 1995 - 1998
REFERENCES:	Available on request.

JANIS DARIEN

345 W. 3rd St.   Telephone: 617/555-3291
Boston, MA 02210

JOB OBJECTIVE:	To obtain a position as a marketing management trainee.
EDUCATION:	Boston University, Boston, MA
	B.A. degree in Economics, June 1997 Dean's list four quarters 3.5 GPA in major field 3.8 GPA overall
	Plan to pursue graduate studies toward a Master's degree in Marketing at Boston University, Evening Division.
WORK EXPERIENCE:	Lewis Advertising Agency, Boston, MA Marketing Assistant, 9/97 to Present
	Assist Marketing Manager in areas of promotion, product development and demographic analysis.
	Paterno Marketing, Boston, MA Telephone Interviewer, Summer 1996
	Conducted telemarketing surveys to help clients analyze demographics and product demand and create marketing strategies.
SPECIAL SKILLS:	Fluent in French. Familiar with WordPerfect, ClarisWorks, Microsoft Works, Lotus1-2-3
REFERENCES:	Available on request.

Christopher Knight
1700 W. Armadillo
San Diego, CA 90087
619/555-9000
619/555-2839

OBJECTIVE: To obtain a position as Vice-President of Public Relations with an aeronautical corporation.

AREAS OF EXPERIENCE:

Marketing Development

*Initiated and supervised sales programs for aircraft distributors selling aircraft to businesses throughout the Western United States.

*Managed accounts with a profit range of $100,000 to $1,000,000, including Dow Chemical, Landston Steel, Mercury Company, Berkeley Metallurgical, and Ford Motor Company.

*Demonstrated to customer companies how to use aircraft to coordinate and consolidate expanding facilities.

*Introduced and expanded use of aircraft for musical tours.

Public Relations

*Handled all levels of sales promotion, corporate public relations, and training of industry on company use of aircraft.

*Managed promotions including personal presentations, radio and TV broadcasts, news stories, and magazine features.

Pilot Training

*Taught primary, secondary, and instrument flight in single and multi-engine aircraft.

Page 1 of 2

Christopher Knight - 2

EMPLOYMENT HISTORY:	Hughes Aircraft, Inc., San Diego, CA Sales Manager and Chief Pilot 1996 to Present
	Boeing Corporation, Kansas City, MO Assistant Manager of Promotion 1987 to 1996
	American Airlines, Dallas, TX Pilot 1980 to 1987
	United States Air Force, Houston, TX Flight Instructor 1978 to 1980
PROFESSIONAL LICENSE:	Airline Transport Rating 14352-60 Single, Multi-Engine Land Flight Instructor - Instrument
EDUCATION:	University of Texas, Houston, TX B.A. in History, 1961
MILITARY SERVICE:	United States Air Force 1975 to 1980
REFERENCES:	Available on request

CARLOS VEGA

548 W. Hollywood Way
Burbank, CA 91505

818/555-9090

Professional Objective:

An upper-level management position in the record industry where I can employ my promotion and marketing experience.

Professional Background:

Warner Brothers Records, Burbank, CA
Director of Marketing/Jazz Department, 1996 to Present

Develop and maintain strategic marketing campaigns for new releases and catalog. Produce reissue packages and samplers, both retail and promotional. Create ad copy. Interface with creative services and national and local print and radio. Oversee all aspects of sales. Coordinate promotional activities and chart reports.

I.R.S. Records, Los Angeles, CA
National Sales Manager, 1992 to 1996
West Coast Sales Manager, 1989 to 1992

Increased sales profile, specifically West Coast retailers, one-stops, and racks. Promoted to national sales manager, where I established sales and promotion programs for company. Coordinated radio/chart reports.

Specialty Records, Scranton, PA
Sales Representative, 1988

Handled sales, merchandising, and account servicing for LPs and cassettes. Called on major chains and small independent retailers. Promoted new releases and maintained account inventory.

Page 1 of 2

Tower Records, Los Angeles, CA
Manager, 1987 to 1988

Handled sales, merchandising, customer service, product selection
and ordering, personnel management and supervision for a full-line
retail outfit.

MCA Records Distribution, Universal City, CA
Sales Representative, 1981 to 1987

Promoted and sold MCA product in Los Angeles and surrounding
counties. Designed in-store and window displays. Coordinated
media advertising support programs.

Education:

Berkeley University, Berkeley, CA
B.A., Liberal Arts, 1981

References Available

CAROL BAKER
4420 Sunset Blvd.
Hollywood, CA 90027
213/555-9098

JOB SOUGHT: Promotion Director for a TV station.

SKILLS AND ACHIEVEMENTS

Promotion/Marketing

*Wrote and designed promotional pieces
*Evaluated content and direction of promotions
*Handled market research/demographic research
*Consulted clients on marketing plans

Video Production

*Handled shooting procedures, audio, lighting, casting, and editing
*Wrote and edited shooting scripts
*Determined production values for marketing accounts
*Oversaw postproduction and placement

Media Planning

*Advised clients on media strategies
*Oversaw media budgets
*Determined and implemented marketing objectives
*Negotiated spot rates for clients

EMPLOYMENT HISTORY

Geary Advertising, Inc., Los Angeles, CA
Media Planner, 1997 to Present

Goebert & Radner, Inc , Chicago, IL
Assistant Media Buyer, 1994 to 1997

Sears, Inc., Chicago, IL
Advertising Assistant, 1992 to 1994

EDUCATION

Drake University, Des Moines, IA
B.A. in Economics, 1992, Phi Beta Kappa
Minor in Advertising

REFERENCES ON REQUEST

JOHNNY KAZELL
5320 Wilshire Blvd.
Los Angeles, CA 90069
213/555-9282

OBJECTIVE: Seeking a marketing position in the music industry.

WORK EXPERIENCE:

Hit Productions, Los Angeles, CA
Public Relations/Marketing Assistant, 5/97 - Present

Assist Public Relations Director with all duties, including radio promotion and retail marketing. Coordinate radio and print interviews for artists. Typing, filing, and answering phones.

KCLA Radio, Los Angeles, CA
Music Director, 6/96 - 5/97

Selected appropriate music for student radio station. Oversaw daily operations of music library and programming department. Supervised staff of six student volunteers.

EDUCATION:

UCLA, Los Angeles, CA
B.A. in Arts Management, May 1997

ACTIVITIES:

Phi Mu Alpha Music Fraternity, President
Alpha Lambda Fraternity

SPECIAL SKILLS:

Working knowledge of Microsoft Word and Lotus 1-2-3.

References available on request.

Jacob Rosenthal
2950 W. Best Road
Raleigh, North Carolina 27695

(303) 442-5284

Community Relations/Media Specialist

Overview

Self-employed communications professional with extensive experience assisting both private and nonprofit agencies to promote their services and maintain a positive image in the community. Diverse experience and skills.

Work History

1996 to Present
Owner, Rosenthal Communications

Manage successful freelance business with clients including the City of Raleigh, Raleigh General Hospital, North Carolina State University, Carleton Community College, and Riverside Amusement Corporation. Design complete publicity packages to inform community of available services, promote corporate identity, and increase sales. Write press releases, brochures, ad copy, feature articles, and statements to press. Produce radio and cable TV spots. Develop concept with client and manage all details while supervising subcontractors as necessary and keeping client abreast of progress.

1994 to 1996
Community Services Director
North Carolina State University

Directed community outreach programs. Conducted needs assessments and worked in conjunction with academic faculty and administrative staff to meet the needs of diverse learners. Created distance learning options and promoted these new programs through local and national media. Arranged off-site course locations for evening division courses.

Page 1 of 2

1992 to 1994
Production Assistant
WNC-TV

Assisted in production of wide variety of community access programming, including children's and educational television. Assisted producers on-site with setups and breakdowns of shoots. Edited footage. Produced promotional spots and public service announcements.

Education

North Carolina State University
B.A. in Communications, 1992

References

References and portfolio of work are available for review.

JAMES ROBERT WEITSMA

1200 Wodler Drive
Apartment 3E
Chicago, IL 60607
Telephone: 312/555-4903

OBJECTIVE: A position as a sales management trainee.

EDUCATION: NORTHWESTERN UNIVERSITY, Evanston, IL

B.A. in Advertising, expected June 1998
Dean's List five quarters
3.6 G.P.A. in major field
3.5 G.P.A. overall

Activities:
Alumni Committee
Student Activities Board

WORK EXPERIENCE: AT&T, Chicago, IL
Sales Intern, 9/97 to Present
Assist sales manager in areas of promotion, product development, and marketing.

HANDELMAN MARKETING, Winnetka, IL
Telephone Surveyor, Summer 1996

YESTERDAY'S, Evanston, IL
Waiter, Summer 1995

SPECIAL SKILLS: Fluent in Spanish.
Familiar with WordPerfect 6.0, ClarisWorks, and Lotus 1-2-3

REFERENCES: Available on request

LISA STANSFIELD

14 E. Three Penny Road
Detroit, MI 33290
313/555-3489

OBJECTIVE

A management position in public relations where I can utilize my promotion and marketing experience.

WORK EXPERIENCE

SEVEN ELEVEN INC., Detroit, MI
Marketing Director, 1995 - present
Developed a successful marketing campaign for a convenience store chain. Initiated and maintained a positive working relationship with radio and print media. Implemented marketing strategies to increase sales at less profitable outlets. Designed a training program for store managers and staff.

SUPER VACUUM COMPANY, Bloomfield Hills, MI
Marketing Representative, 1991 - 1995
Demonstrated vacuums in specialty and department stores. Reported customer reactions to manufacturers. Designed fliers and advertising to promote products. Made frequent calls to retail outlets.

REBO CARPETS, INC., Chicago, IL
Assistant to Sales Manager, 1986 - 1991
Handled both internal and external areas of sales and marketing, including samples, advertising, and pricing. Served as company sales representative and sold carpeting to retail outlets.

EDUCATION

UNIVERSITY OF MICHIGAN, Ann Arbor, MI
B.A. Marketing, 1987

SEMINARS

Michigan Marketing Workshop, 1997, 1998
Sales and Marketing Association Seminars, 1993

References available on request.

LINDA MAXWELL
916 Rockport Road
Phoenix, AZ 85016

~~~~

Internet: Maxit.com
602-555-9136 (day)
602-555-6868 (evenings)

OBJECTIVE: **Marketing Executive**

WORK HISTORY:

9/96 to Present
Marketing Manager
Southwest Publishing, Phoenix

Duties: Direct publisher's marketing efforts. Responsible for producing catalogs and direct mail pieces. Coordinate with advertising department. Track sales histories and design pricing and promotional strategies. Hire, train, and supervise sales staff. Represent publisher at sales conventions, industry trade shows. Liaison to wholesalers and distributors.

5/93 to 8/96
Advertising Copywriter
Current Communications, Inc., Phoenix

Duties: Produced ad copy and brochures. Designed, produced, and distributed direct mail packages.

Telemarketer
6/92 to 5/93
TDK Marketing, Dallas

Duties: Conducted phone surveys to research consumer preferences and purchase patterns. Compiled results and drafted reports.

                              Page 1 of 2

Linda Maxwell
-2-

EDUCATION:

B.S. in Communications
University of Arizona
June 1992

MEMBERSHIPS:

American Marketing Association
National Association of Women in Business

REFERENCES:

Portfolio and complete list of references supplied on request.

LUIS CASTILLO
8155 N. KNOX
SKOKIE, IL 60076
708/555-3168

JOB OBJECTIVE: Sales position where I can utilize my retail sales, cash management, and supervisory skills.

WORK EXPERIENCE:

Gateway, Inc., Chicago, IL
Manager/Salesperson, 11/96 - Present

Manage own jewelry business. Sell jewelry at wholesale and retail levels. Negotiate prices with customers. Handle all finances and bookkeeping.

West Miami Jewelry, Miami, FL
Manager, 1/93 - 11/96

Managed a retail jewelry store. Oversaw all aspects of sales, purchasing, and bookkeeping. Supervised two employees.

EDUCATION:

Interamerica Business Institute, Chicago, IL 2/97 - present
Major: Business Management

Northeastern University, Chicago, IL
Attended 1991- 1993
Area of concentration: Business Management

References available on request.

Peter Simmons
678 Park Street #546
Noblesville, IN 46060
(219) 555-6042

OBJECTIVE:

To obtain an executive position in marketing with an emerging company that is dedicated to a long-term program.

EXPERIENCE:

5/95-Present DCS SOFTWARE, INC. Noblesville, IN
Senior Partner
Contingency Marketing Agency

-Designed marketing strategies for local and national companies
-Directly responsible for meeting payroll of 25 full-time employees
-Improved sales for one company by over 25% in a 12-month period
-Developed marketing programs for corporations

1/94-5/95 BLAUVELT ENGINEERS, New York, NY

Regional Sales Manager
Business Communications Systems

-Set regional sales record in six months
-Procured ten national accounts
-Exceeded company goals for the 1994 fiscal year
-Developed sales marketing program for the northwest regional area

8/90-1/94 EDWARDS AND KELCEY, Livingston, NJ

Marketing Director

-Implemented international marketing program
-Promoted from sales executive to marketing director
-Company's sales increased over 100% in a 12-month span
-Successful in developing database and reselling to them directly

EDUCATION: Stevens Institute of Technology, NJ
Bachelors of Arts Degree in the area of Technical Marketing Design

REFERENCES AVAILABLE

Mark Ho
P.O. Box 22
Boston, Massachusetts 02125
(617) 555 - 9876

OBJECTIVE   Key executive position in marketing management or general management.

SUMMARY   Fifteen years of diverse, multi-disciplinary management experience with broad-based exposure and expertise in the various facets of marketing, operations, sales, and general management.

    Demonstrated ability to profitably expand mature business and to manage corporate assets for optimum productivity. Proven analytical, conceptual, and people skills.

EDUCATION

MBA (Marketing)	1995	University of Massachusetts
Masters (Mathematics)	1990	Williams College
B.B. (Mathematics)	1988	Williams College

EXPERIENCE

CADD CONVERSION   VICE PRESIDENT
DIRECTOR OF MARKETING
1994 to Present

* Reversed the 25% decline in unit sales volume in the two-year period preceding employment. Increased unit sales volume 25% and total sales revenue 75% in the subsequent two-year period.

* Developed marketing strategies to exploit existing product opportunities in present and new markets, i.e. commercial, industrial, institutional, and plan/spec. Strategies focused on an expanded product line with exclusive options and different product features; multiple model selections; and complementary new products.

* Conceptualized and implemented an aggressive product diversification effort. Supplementary HVAC products were acquired on a representation basis and now comprise approximately 50% of total sales revenue.

* Established a national sales representation network to market industrial/commercial ceiling fans and air handling, air cleaning, heating, and ventilation equipment.

* Identified and developed private label accounts in three new markets, i.e. agricultural, church, and direct mail, resulting in a 25% increase in private label unit sales volume.

Page 1 of 2

Mark Ho
Page 2 of 2

TECTONIC SOFTWARE SYSTEMS   BUSINESS DEVELOPMENT MANAGER
1990 to 1994

* Identified and exploited complementary business opportunities in new but related markets resulting in a 15% increase in special OEM Bales.

* Devised a simplified marketing strategy to upgrade, restructure, and optimize the performance of mature strategic business units.

* Developed comprehensive business assessments relative to participation in high growth, high profit consumer, and industrial product markets.

* Assumed a leading role in the identification, strategic assessment, and financial analysis of complementary business acquisitions.

MULTIFRAME   MARKETING MANAGER
PRODUCT MANAGER
1988 to 1990

* Created a $25M new market by modifying an existing product to meet specific customer needs in the software system for Macintosh.

* Managed the successful launch of two new "engineered" products for the software industry and eliminated outdated product lines.

* Supervised an innovative and persuasive advertising/sales promotion program to create demand for engineered products at the OEM level and to exploit burgeoning after-market sales opportunities.

REFERENCES AVAILABLE

YVONNE KORBIN
33 E. Lincoln
Chicago, IL 60655
Tel. (312) 555-2029
Fax (312) 555-4394

GOAL:	A marketing/publicity position in the recording industry.
WORK HISTORY:	PTO PRODUCTION, Evanston IL Public Relations/Marketing Assistant Dates: 5/97 to Present
	Duties: Assist Public Relations Director with all duties, including radio promotion and retail marketing. Coordinate radio and print interviews for artists. Manage all details of office including scheduling, record keeping, and document preparation.
	WCHO RADIO, Chicago, IL Music Director Dates: 6/96 to 5/97
	Duties: Selected appropriate music for a contemporary jazz format. Oversaw daily operations of music library and programming department. Supervised a staff of six.
EDUCATION:	Northwestern University, Evanston, IL B.A. in Arts Management, May 1997
	G.P.A. in major: 3.8
	Received Ross Hunter Arts Management Scholarship
SKILLS:	Fluent in French Working knowledge of WordPerfect 6.0 and Lotus 1-2-3

References on Request

WINONA T. SIMPSON
420 W. Easterly Avenue
Indianapolis, IN 49091
317/555-1212

OBJECTIVE

A management position in marketing or public relations.

PROFESSIONAL ACHIEVEMENTS

Marketing/Public Relations

* Developed a successful marketing campaign for a video rental chain.
* Initiated and maintained a positive working relationship with radio and print media.
* Implemented marketing strategies to increase sales at less profitable stores.
* Designed a training program for store managers and staff.

Promotion

* Demonstrated electronic equipment in stereo and department stores.
* Reported customer reactions to manufacturers.
* Designed fliers and advertising to promote products.

EMPLOYMENT HISTORY

Blockbuster Video, Inc., Indianapolis, IN
Public Relations Director, 1990-Present

Jeron Stereo, Bloomington, IN
Marketing Representative, 1987-1990

Kader Advertising, St. Louis, MO
Public Relations Assistant, 1985-1987

EDUCATION

Washington University, St. Louis, MO
B.S. in Education, 1985

HONORS

Phi Beta Kappa, 1985
Top 5% of class
Dean's List

REFERENCES

Provided on request

RITA WESTERBURG

3201 W. Oerono St.
Apartment 23
Pittsburgh, PA 28901
412-555-9302 (office)
412-555-4209 (home)

JOB SOUGHT: Public relations director for the marketing division of a major candy manufacturer.

**RELEVANT
EXPERIENCE:**

Public Relations

-Represented company to clients and retailers in order to present new products.
-Organized and planned convention displays and strategy.
-Designed and executed direct mail campaign that identified marketplace needs
 and new options for products.

Management

-Managed a sales/marketing staff that included account managers and sales
 representatives.
-Monitored and studied the effectiveness of a national distribution network.
-Oversaw all aspects of sales/marketing budget.

Development

-Conceived ads, posters, and point-of-purchase materials for products.
-Initiated and published a monthly newsletter that was distributed to current and
 potential customers.

**EMPLOYMENT
HISTORY:**

Redboy Peanut Crunch, Pittsburgh, PA
National Sales Manager, 1995 - present
Account Manager, 1993 - 1995
Assistant Account Manager, 1992 - 1993
Personnel Assistant, 1990 - 1992
Receptionist, 1988 - 1990

EDUCATION:

B.A. in English, May 1988
University of Pennsylvania, Harrisburg, PA

SEMINARS:

American Marketing Association Seminars, 1992 - 1997

**SPECIAL
SKILLS:**

Computer literacy in BASIC and FORTRAN. Knowledge of WordPerfect 6.0
and dBase III.

REFERENCES:

Available on request

DIANNE BROWNSKI

3355 Brookshire Parkway, Chicago, IL 60636 ~ Telephone (312) 555-4948 ~ Fax (312) 555-4897

OBJECTIVE: I hope to utilize my communication, problem-solving, and decision-making skills in a sales and marketing position with opportunities for advancement.

EDUCATION: ITT Business Institute, Associate Degree in Sales and Marketing, June 1997

EXPERIENCE:

5/97 to Present	**Marketing Assistant**	**SERVICE SOFTWARE INC.**

Develop and implement marketing strategies for software design firm. Assist advertising department with ad copy. Write, edit, and proofread catalog copy and user manuals. Write direct-mail pieces.

6/95 to 5/97	**Executive Secretary**	**NEW WORLD PACKAGING**

Responsible for clerical and receptionist duties for packaging firm. Maintained all office files and records. Produced correspondence. Directed all incoming calls. Provided basic customer service.

SKILLS: WordPerfect 6.1, Excel
Typing Speed of 70 w.p.m.
Ten-key Calculator by Touch
Some knowledge of Spanish

REFERENCES AVAILABLE

Stacey Charles
609 Lincoln Road
Houston, Texas 77386
(713) 555-1947

OBJECTIVE

Management trainee position dealing with the sales
and/or marketing of computer hardware and software.

EDUCATION

Baylor University
BS in Marketing expected June 1999
Minor in Computer Science with coursework in
COBOL, BASIC, RPG II, Pascal, and C

GPA of 4.9/5.0

Earned 50% of tuition by working while carrying full
course load.

EMPLOYMENT

1996-Present   Computer Lab Assistant, Baylor
                      University

Instruct undergraduates in use of computer hardware and
software. Assistance ranges from word-processing
instruction to programming assignments.

Summers, 1996-1997 Sales Associate, Computer World

Sold computer equipment and software. Answered customers'
questions. Provided ongoing customer service and training.

REFERENCES AVAILABLE

RHONDA WARONKER

5320 Wilshire Blvd.
Los Angeles, CA 90069
213/555-9282

OBJECTIVE: Seeking a publicity/marketing position in the communications industry.

WORK
EXPERIENCE: WRT Records, Los Angeles, CA
Marketing Director, 9/96-present
Handle distribution, retail marketing, advertising, and mail order marketing. Write
biographies and coordinate publicity. Obtain knowledge regarding domestic and overseas
independent distribution, buyers for U.S. chain stores, and Billboard reporters.

Hit Productions, Los Angeles, CA
Public Relations/Marketing Assistant, 5/95-9/96
Assisted Public Relations Director with all duties, including radio promotion and retail
marketing. Coordinated radio and print interviews for artists. Typing, filing, and
answering phones.

KTWV Radio, Los Angeles, CA
Music Director, 6/94-5/95
Selected appropriate music for a contemporary jazz format. Oversaw daily operations
of music library and programming department. Supervised a staff of six.

EDUCATION: UCLA, Los Angeles, CA
B.A. in Arts Management, June 1994

ACTIVITIES: Phi Mu Alpha Music Fraternity, President
National Association of College Activities
Alpha Lambda Fraternity

SKILLS: Working knowledge of Microsoft Word and Lotus 1-2-3.

References Available

Chapter Six

SAMPLE COVER LETTERS

Kenneth Thomas Parker
1400 Lake Shore Drive
Chicago, IL 60601
(312) 555-6999

May 11, 19--

Ms. Sandra Watt
Human Resources
Porter Sporting Goods, Inc.
133 W. York Avenue
Schiller Park, IL 60027

Dear Ms. Watt:

Is Porter Sporting Goods, Inc. in need of a dedicated, talented sales manager? If so, please consider the enclosed resume.

I am currently employed as assistant sales manager for Wilson Sporting Goods; I've been with the company since 1995. My experience in sporting good sales includes cold calls and visits to retailers that resulted in increased accounts for Wilson. In addition, I pride myself on conducting extensive research into competitors' products in order to create and implement successful marketing strategies.

My research has included Porter Sporting Goods products, and I am impressed by their high quality. I have always admired your company's insight and innovation and would like to put my skills to work for you.

I will call early next week to determine if an interview is appropriate at this time. Thank you for considering my credentials.

Sincerely,

Kenneth Thomas Parker

March 14, 19--

Hollywood Reporter
Box 1140-H
465 Hollywood Way
Burbank, CA 91505

Dear Recruiter:

I am responding to your ad in *The Hollywood Reporter* of February 14th
for a marketing executive. My resume and salary requirements are enclosed,
as you requested.

As my resume indicates, I am a recent graduate of California State University
at Northridge where I received a B.A. in Business. My work experience
includes an internship at Warner Bros. Studios in Burbank, where I worked in
the market research department.

I know that your marketing staff could make good use of my current skills, and
I would consider it a privilege to join an organization with such high standing
in the entertainment industry.

If you wish to schedule an interview, you can reach me at 213-555-7649
between 8 and 4. Or, you may phone me at my home number, 213-555-3333.
Thank you for your time and consideration.

Sincerely,

Ken Phillips
2233 Effingham Place
Los Angeles CA 90027

Moses Washington
1723 Irving Park Road
Chicago, IL 60625
312/555-8928

January 21, 19--

ATTN: Joe Perlman
        Sales Manager
        Shasta, Inc.
        45 E. Huron Street
        Chicago, IL 60623

Dear Mr. Perlman:

The notice you placed on the company bulletin board for a sales coordinator seems
to describe my skills and experience exactly. Therefore, I would like to formally
apply for the position.

As you know, I have been working here at Shasta for the last three years as a sales
representative. My responsibilities have included selling our products to retail outlets,
handling customer requests, and training new sales staff. Working at Shasta has
been a challenge; I've learned a great deal during the last few years and feel well
qualified to take the next step in my career here: becoming the new sales coordinator.

I would like to set up an interview at your convenience. You can reach me at
extension 4222 or at home at 312-555-8928. I look forward to hearing from you
regarding this opportunity.

Sincerely,

Moses Washington

December 11, 19--

David Bascombe III
Sears & Roebuck, Inc.
1000 S. Adams
Chicago, IL 60601

Dear Mr. Bascombe:

I am responding to your job listing for a marketing management trainee that was listed in the placement office at Boston University. My resume is enclosed.

I have recently been graduated from Boston University with a degree in Economics, and I am anxious to find a position in marketing. Eventually, I plan to continue my education, by working toward a master's degree in marketing during the evenings.

My work experience includes employment as a marketing assistant for Lewis Advertising Agency in Boston and a job as a telephone surveyor for Paterno Marketing.

I will be in the Chicago area the week of the 20th. Would it be possible to set up an interview with you during that week? If so, please contact me at 617/555-3291.

Thanks for your time and consideration.

Sincerely,

Janis Darien
345 W. Third Street, #42
Boston, MA 02210

JAMES KENDALL
509 27th Street
New York, NY 10019

May 24, 19--

Paterson and Company
111 W. Monroe Street
Chicago, IL 60660
Attn: David Snowheart

Dear Mr. Snowheart:

A fellow broker at Jones and Jones recently informed me that you have a current opening on your staff for a commodity broker. Therefore I have taken the liberty of sending my resume for your consideration.

I have been in the commodities business for the past fifteen years. During that time, I gained experience as a trader, a sales representative, and finally as a broker for Jones and Jones in New York. I currently handle more than 500 clients as a specialist in corn and wheat futures. I also publish and distribute a weekly newsletter on futures.

In the late 1970s, I worked for Pickering, Pickering & Gold in Chicago; I enjoy Chicago and would be willing to relocate there.

I will be in Chicago early next month and would be glad to meet with you then to discuss this job opening in greater detail. I am most easily reached between 9 and 11 at 212-555-9809. Please feel free to phone me at home in the evening (at 212-555-7777) if that is more convenient.

Sincerely,

James Kendall

JEREMY S. PANDY
1441 S. GOEBERT
PROVIDENCE, RI 00231

June 2, 19--

Anderson Publishing Inc.
1000 Seventh Avenue
Suite 1000
New York, NY 10019
Attn: Delores Darnell
          Director of Personnel

Dear Ms. Darnell:

Through your recent press release, I became aware of the departure of your company's president, Myron Strickland. With that in mind, I am forwarding my resume to you for your consideration in your search for a new president.

With more than twenty years of experience in the publishing industry, including my most current position as vice-president of advertising at Johnson Publishing in Providence, I feel that I have the experience and the industry knowledge to tackle this challenge. My employment history also includes stints with Rebus Publishing and Time Magazine.

I believe that Anderson Publishing is a company with a future, and I am convinced that I can help shape that future. I expect great things from myself and Anderson.

I will be following up this letter with a telephone call next week. I will be in New York City during the week of March 20th and would be happy to meet with you regarding this position at that time.

Thank you for your kind consideration.

Sincerely,

Jeremy S. Pandy
401/555-1234

CAROL A. BADEN
150 W. Fort Washington Avenue
New York, NY 10032
212/555-2498

Dana Jacobs
Human Resources
AT&T
1000 E. 5th Avenue
New York, NY 10090

Dear Mr. Jacobs:

David Sanderson, who works in the marketing department of AT&T, suggested that I contact you regarding a possible management trainee position in your sales department. I am enclosing my resume for your consideration.

I will be graduated this month from New York University with a degree in Communications. I was recently inducted into the Communications Honor Society (Beta Alpha Psi), and I am a member of the Association for International Business (A.I.S.E.C.).

AT&T would be an excellent place for me to start my career in the communications industry, and I would bring a strong academic background and work ethic to the position of management trainee.

I will call early next week to follow up on this letter. Mr. Sanderson would be glad to have you call him for a reference if you like.

Sincerely,

Carol A. Baden

May 15, 19--

Deborah Klugh
Director of Human Resources
NBC
1220 Rockefeller Plaza
New York, NY 10019

Dear Ms. Klugh:

This letter is in response to your ad in the *New York Times* for a sales assistant. My resume and salary requirements are enclosed, as you requested.

Next month I will be graduating from Boston University with a degree in Business Administration and a concentration in sales management. I was inducted into Phi Beta Kappa this month and expect to graduate with honors in June.

I am interested in working in the television industry in a sales capacity and would be pleased to be part of the NBC team.

I would enjoy presenting my qualifications in person, and am willing to travel to New York for an interview. Meanwhile, thank you for your time and consideration.

Sincerely,

Barton T. Quigley
Boston University
Fenton Hall
199 W. Hampshire Way
Boston, MA 02201
612/555-3839

SALLY JOHNSON
3240 Santa Monica Blvd.
Los Angeles, CA 90028

June 11, 19--

David G. Sandler
Director of Human Resources
Nessex Motor Company
1200 Wilshire Blvd.
Santa Monica, CA 90390

Dear Mr. Sandler:

I am interested in applying for the position of assistant manager at your Nessex dealership in Santa Monica. Your ad in last Sunday's *L.A. Times* alerted me to the opening.

Currently, I am a sales representative for Yugo in Los Angeles. My duties there, besides sales, include market analyses, research, forecasts, and resolution of sales and billing problems.

Although I enjoy my current job, which I've held for three years, I am always interested in exploring new challenges in auto sales. The job of assistant manager at your dealership would be such a challenge, and I think my background would make me a real asset to your sales team.

My resume is enclosed for your review. I appreciate your consideration and look forward to interviewing with you.

Sincerely,

Sally Johnson
213/555-9832 (Home)
213/555-2121 (Work)

April 17, 19--

Robert T. Beatty
Director of Personnel
Turner Broadcasting Co.
One Turner Plaza
Atlanta, GA 33203

Dear Mr. Beatty:

Thank you for taking time today to discuss openings at Turner Broadcasting. As I mentioned,
I am most interested in working for the company in the area of advertising sales.

Here is the resume you requested. You will note that I have several years of sales experience,
including work for Medialink Advertising Agency in San Francisco and KTUT-TV in Portland.
These previous positions have given me a strong background in media sales. In particular,
my employers seem to appreciate my ability to assess the content and suitabilty of ads
and to analyze demographic data.

My current goal is to pursue a job in cable television, so I appreciate your willingness to
review my resume and inform me of any suitable opening at Turner. I will call early next week
to discuss whether an interview is in order.

Meanwhile, thanks for your time and encouragement.

Sincerely yours,

Sandra T. Peterson
12 E. Tenth Street
San Francisco, CA 97890
415/555-2343

BELINDA CARLISLE
333 E. 20th St. #3
New York, NY 10019
212/555-2902

December 2, 19--

Corlis Fenett, Jr.
President
Venture Publishing Corporation
7 Rockefeller Plaza
New York, NY 10019

Dear Mr. Fenett:

As regional marketing manager of *Coast Magazine,* I have faced many challenges and have handled each of them thoroughly, responsibly, and efficiently. I have learned and contributed a great deal to the magazine. In this position, I oversee all sales and marketing efforts, and the hiring and training of sales staff. I have led the magazine's Eastern edition through a difficult reorganization period and planned and implemented new marketing strategies for the South.

I have enjoyed my tenure at *Coast,* but I feel it is time to move on to a new challenge. This challenge, I hope, will be the position of Director of Sales and Marketing at Venture Publishing Corporation. I learned of this opening from a colleague in publishing.

My resume is enclosed. Please review it and contact me if you are interested. I am confident that you will be.

Sincerely,

Belinda Carlisle

JOHN L. RYDER
211 W. Fourth Street
Brooklyn, NY 10001
718/555-9080

April 18, 19--

John Junot
Fidelity Insurance Company
1440 W. 57th Street
New York, NY 10019

Dear Mr. Junot:

I am responding to your advertisement for an East Coast Sales Manager, which appeared in the April 15th issue of the *Financial News*. As you asked, I am enclosing my resume and a list of references.

After several years working as an agent and an adjustor, I feel I am ready to make the move into a sales management position. I believe that a position of this kind at Fidelity would benefit both me and the company. My extensive experience in the insurance industry has prepared me well for this next step in my career.

I would enjoy discussing my credentials and your current needs in greater detail. I will call early next week to discuss if and when you would like to schedule an interview.

Cordially,

John L. Ryder

**Johanna Farac
152 S. Fedner Drive
Omaha, NE 73802**

February 13, 19--

Dear Ms. Evers:

I was intrigued by your ad in the *Omaha Register* for a management trainee for your bookstore, and I've enclosed the resume and salary requirements you requested.

All of my life I've been fascinated by books and bookstores. In high school I worked in the student bookstore for four years. My work experience also includes stints as a salesperson for Fern Books and as assistant sales manager for Crown Books in Omaha.

I would enjoy the challenge of applying this experience at Federated Books. Your current needs and my interests seem to match well.

I will call early next week to discuss arranging an interview. Thank you for your time and consideration.

Sincerely,

Johanna Farac
401/555-9000 (Day)
401/555-6712 (Evening)

DAVID P. JENKINS

3663 N. Coldwater Canyon
North Hollywood, CA 90390
818/555-3472

July 23, 19---

Mr. Jeremy Hitleman
Vice President, Sales and Marketing
Sandoval Industries
500 University Drive
Santa Barbara, CA 87809

Dear Mr. Hitleman:

I am writing to you to inquire about the possibility of obtaining a position with Sandoval Industries as a sales/marketing manager.

My special interest in working for your company stems from a desire to expand my experience into the area of hardware sales. Your company's recent addition of a hardware division brought Sandoval to my attention.

Currently, I serve as regional sales manager for Tribor Industries where I represent five corporate divisions with sales in excess of three million annually. Previous to this position, I served as district manager for Tribor.

I believe that my sales experience well qualifies me for a position at Sandoval Industries. I hope that reviewing the enclosed resume will convince you of the same.

Thanks for your consideration. I am available at your convenience if you wish to schedule an interview.

Sincerely,

David P. Jenkins

JERRY MATHEWS, JR.
6701 W. Mariposa Ave.
Boise, ID 83209
(919) 555-3402

August 18, 19--

Paul H. Harrison
Vice President of Marketing
Boise Electronic Corporation
4000 N. Agricultural Blvd.
Boise, ID 84203

Dear Mr. Harrison:

Boise Electronic has been enjoying tremendous success and growth over the last few years; your company is rapidly becoming a leader in the home electronics field. I am certain that a key factor in that success is a talented sales staff. That is why I am sure that my resume will be of interest to you.

I have seven years of experience in sales with three different companies. Currently, I am a sales assistant with Codaphone, Inc., a company that sells telephone equipment. My position there involves both sales and servicing accounts. Both clients and my employer tell me that they value my customer service, communication, and sales skills--qualities that may be equally valuable to Boise Electronic.

Would you like to meet to discuss my qualifications further? I will call next week to discuss any current openings you may have. Thank you for your time.

Sincerely,

Jerry Mathews, Jr.

WINONA T. SIMPSON
420 W. Easterly Avenue
Indianapolis, IN 49091

June 23, 19--

Thomas E. Eagletender
Pizza Hut, Inc.
4200 Bolt Avenue
Indianapolis, IN 49091

Dear Mr. Eagletender:

David Porter of your marketing department informed me that you were looking for a new marketing manager for your midwest office. Therefore, I am sending along my resume so that I may be considered for this position.

Currently, I serve as marketing director for Blockbuster Video in Indianapolis. Before that I was a marketing representative for Jeron Stereo and a marketing assistant for Kader Advertising.

My accomplishments include developing a successful marketing campaign for Blockbuster, implementing marketing strategies to increase sales at less profitable outlets, and designing a training program for store managers and staff.

As soon as you have had a chance to review my resume, I would like to meet with you to discuss this position further. You can reach me at 317/555-1212. Thank you for considering my credentials.

Yours truly,

Winona T. Simpson

October 9, 19--

Felicia Robertson
Gandy's Fine Jewelry
2300 S. Vermont Ave.
Los Angeles, CA 90380

Dear Ms. Robertson:

James Gooden, who works at your store, suggested that I send you a resume. I would like to be considered for any upcoming sales positions at Gandy's. I have always wanted to work for Gandy's because I believe it to be the best fine jewelry store in southern California.

My experience includes sales work at Stacey's Jewelers in Chatsworth and at Eddy Gems in Glendale. My skills include greeting customers, advising them on purchases, and designing window displays.

I am available at your convenience if you are interested in scheduling an interview. Thank you for considering me.

Sincerely,

Melanie B. Maloney
1200 Puerta Del Sol
Chatsworth, CA 92203
714/555-6789

Steven R. Stevens
Red Man Furnace Company
7892 Collins Ave.
Miami, FL 08902

Dear Mr. Stevens:

I am forwarding my resume in response to the advertisement for a sales manager that you placed in the August 18th issue of the *Miami Herald*.

As my resume indicates, I have extensive sales experience that goes back ten years. As an account executive for Newmark Furnace Company, I have handled sales accounts in the south Florida area and expanded my customer base by 28% in the last three years. Prior to that, I worked as a sales representative for Potisco in Terre Haute, Indiana, and for Honoco, in Chicago.

I feel confident that I could do an outstanding job as your new sales manager, and I would welcome the opportunity to discuss the opening in person. I am available at your convenience if you would like to arrange an interview.

Sincerely,

Patrick H. McCoy
1701 N. Hampshire Place
Miami, FL 03908
305/555-3909
305/555-9099

GINA CAROL STONE
5001 Lincoln Drive #2
Marlton, NJ 08053
609/555-1200
609/555-3893

August 3, 19--

Mr. Howard G. Flagellum
Director of Personnel
Best Paper Products
500 E. Third Street, Suite 1000
Trenton, NJ 08390

Dear Mr. Flagellum:

Are you interested in finding new, more effective ways to motivate your sales staff? If so, I think my resume will interest you.

As district sales manager for Harrison Paper Company in Philadelphia, I have developed valuable skills that well qualify me for a management position in your company. After seven years at Harrison, I am ready for a change, but I want to continue working within the paper products industry.

Some of my accomplishments at Harrison include increased sales each year, supervision of seven sales representatives, and extensive market research that led to the establishment of several major new accounts.

I am free to interview at any time. Please let me know if you are hiring in this area. Thank you for your time and consideration.

Cordially,

Gina Carol Stone